First published by Fairfield Books in 2022

fairfield books

Fairfield Books
Wildfire Sport
Bedser Stand
Kia Oval
London
SE11 5SS

Typeset in Garamond
Typesetting by Rob Whitehouse

Every effort has been made to trace copyright and any oversight
will be rectified in future editions at the earliest opportunity

The views and opinions expressed in this book are those of the
author and do not necessarily reflect the views of the publishers

© 2022 Kit Harris
ISBN 978-1-915237-19-4

A CIP catalogue record for is available from the British Library

THE QUEEN
AT THE CRICKET

KIT HARRIS

Contents

Introduction

Very few of us can say, or will ever be able to say, that we've been going to the cricket for 67 years. Still fewer have been to a Test match in each of eight decades. But Queen Elizabeth II, monarch of the United Kingdom of Great Britain and Northern Ireland for 70 years, managed to squeeze more international cricket into her reign than most of us manage in our rather less busy or prominent lives.

Less busy? That seems a bold statement. But look at her diary for 29 May 2019, the day on which she received the World Cup captains at Buckingham Palace. Before the reception, she had already met two Poets Laureate, and Canadian military top brass. After the cricketers left, she hosted a garden party for 8,000 members of the community, before conducting her weekly meeting with the Prime Minister. She was 94 years old – and this was by no means an unusual day. There was no end to a life's work for the Queen.

The cricketer's life span, and the Queen's longevity, meant she saw hundreds of them play, including almost all the household names of their time. She saw Compton and Edrich bat (and bowl), Trueman and Tyson hit the deck, Laker and Underwood spin their spells, Anderson and Broad charging in.

The Queen attended 44 cricket matches, including 36 trips to Lord's, 35 Tests, 12 England victories, and one World Cup final. She went to London, Adelaide, Melbourne, Bridgetown, Rawalpindi (and Guildford). She may not have been a lucky charm against the Old Enemy – her results as a spectator were six to Australia, one to England and four draws – but, against all other opponents, England never lost a match she visited.

This book tells the story of every match the Queen attended. A whistlestop tour, if you will, through English cricket, as she saw it. But there are not only matches here. From receptions to openings, from knighthoods to peerages, you will find much else besides.

Kit Harris
Shepperton, 2022

First play for the Princess

England v South Africa at Lord's, 1947

England 554 for 8 declared (D. C. S. Compton 208, W. J. Edrich 189, C. Washbrook 65; L. T. D. Tuckett 5–115) **and 26 for 0**. **South Africa 327** (A. Melville 117, A. D. Nourse 61; D. V. P. Wright 5–95) **and 252** (B. Mitchell 80, A. D. Nourse 58; D. V. P. Wright 5–80). **England won by 10 wickets.**

The first Test, at Nottingham, had been drawn. South Africa racked up 533, with twin centuries for Alan Melville – the first South African to achieve the feat in a Test – and a hundred for Dudley Nourse. England collapsed, falling from 154 for two to 208 all out. Bill Edrich and Denis Compton – in the middle of the famous season in which they scored 7,355 runs between them – made half-centuries, but seamer Lindsay Tuckett took 5 for 68. Following on 325 behind, England made a better fist of things in their second innings. Compton hit 163, and captain Norman Yardley reached a Test-best 99; they set South Africa 227 to win, but time was running out. Melville achieved his record, but stumps were drawn with the visitors 61 short.

At Lord's, England won the toss and decided to bat first. Len Hutton and Cyril Washbrook were both out before 100 was raised, but then came a mammoth partnership: Edrich and Compton put on 370, still England's third-wicket record in Tests. After Edrich fell, Compton – hooking, pulling and sweeping imperiously – reached a career-best 208, before Tuckett's pace and hostility were rewarded by some declaration batting, giving him another five-wicket haul. England closed their innings at 554 and, by the end of the second day, South Africa were 167 for two, having lost Bruce Mitchell, stumped by Godfrey Evans off Compton, and Ken Viljoen, bowled by Doug Wright's quicker ball. Melville, despite being struck over the right eye by a throw from the outfield, was 96 not out overnight, having put on 63 for the third wicket with Nourse.

Third day – 24 June

It was the first official visit by HRH The Princess Elizabeth to a cricket match; she was 21 years old, would be engaged two weeks later, and married in November. She saw England leg-spinner Doug Wright take four wickets, part of his only 10-wicket Test. South Africa's Alan Melville, a supremely elegant batter but almost unable to see out of a black eye sustained the previous day, reached his third century in successive innings, but his team followed on. Dudley Nourse hit twin half-centuries, and Princess Elizabeth got to see Denis Compton and Bill Edrich bowl – but not bat. Alec Bedser, who would receive an OBE in 1964, a CBE in 1982 and a knighthood in 1997, went wicketless in both innings.

Lord's had a capacity crowd, with 30,000 spectators, and the day was initially South Africa's. Melville reached his century from the fourth ball of the morning, though he then slowed, since his bruised eye had almost completely closed up. The pair extended their stand to 118 before Eric Hollies had Melville caught pulling by Alec Bedser with the score on 222. Eight runs later, Nourse was lbw to Wright, but Ossie Dawson and Tony Harris added another 60. Harris then became a second stumping victim for Evans off Compton, and the visitors' collapse began in earnest. Charlie Barnett caught Dawson off Hollies; Wright bowled Athol Rowan, Tufty Mann and Tuckett, finishing with five wickets. Having lost six for 37, South Africa were all out for 327, and Yardley asked them to bat again. Inevitably, he soon brought Wright on, but it was Edrich, bowling a great pace at second change, who got England moving, knocking out Melville's middle stump and doing the same to Viljoen. Mitchell and Nourse rebuilt, and took their second-wicket partnership to 92 by the close: South Africa were 120 for two, with Nourse on 58, his second half-century of the match.

Edrich got Nourse second ball next morning, but Dawson knuckled down again, adding 72 with Mitchell, who reached 80 before there was a double breakthrough at 192: Edrich dived full-length at second slip to hold Mitchell off Wright, then caught

Dawson off Compton. Nine runs later, Compton removed Harris, caught by Yardley. A second collapse was just around the corner: at 227 for six, Wright once again found big spin, claiming a second five-wicket haul, and match figures of 10 for 175. England needed just 26 to take a lead in the series.

Edrich dominated England's seven-wicket victory in the third Test at Old Trafford, making 191 in the first innings, and taking eight for 172 in the match. The series was sealed with a ten-wicket win in the fourth Test at Headingley, Hutton scoring 100 and 32 not out, and Ken Cranston ending South Africa's second innings with four wickets in six balls. The fifth Test at The Oval was drawn, with a century for Compton, and twin centuries (120 and 189 not out) for Mitchell. By the end of the tour, Melville's powers had waned: he was exhausted and under-nourished (rationing was still in force in England), and announced his retirement.

The cross-Pennine spin twins

England v South Africa at Lord's, 1951

England 311 (D. C. S. Compton 79, W. Watson 79, J. T. Ikin 51; G. W.
A. Chubb 5–77, C. N. McCarthy 4–76) **and 16 for 0. South Africa 115**
(R. Tattersall 7–52) **and 211** (G. M. Fullerton 60, J. E. Cheetham 54;
R. Tattersall 5–49). **England won by 10 wickets.**

South Africa won the first Test, at Nottingham, thus ending their
run of 28 Tests without victory, going back to 1935. The hero was
Nourse, who batted with a broken thumb to score 208 in 555 minutes,
spending almost all of the first two days at the crease. Replying to
483, England fought hard, and were 375 for 3 at one stage, Reg
Simpson and Compton both scoring hundreds. South Africa chipped
away for a lead of 64, despite Bedser's 6 for 37. England needed
just 186 for a fifth-day win, but by then the pitch was encouraging
prodigious spin: off-spinner Athol Rowan and slow left-armer Mann
shared nine wickets as the hosts fell well short.

Thus England were chasing the series when they arrived in St
John's Wood. They won the toss and batted, and though they
slipped to 103 for 3 after Jack Ikin's spirited half-century, Compton
and Willie Watson wrested back control with a fourth-wicket stand
of 122. South Africa's opening bowlers, the quick Cuan McCarthy
and the swing expert Geoff Chubb, returned to stop England from
completely dominating the day; Chubb worked his way through the
lower order to claim five wickets for the first time in Tests. South
Africa were 4 for 0 at the close.

Second day – 22 June

**Aged 25 and married, HRH The Princess Elizabeth, now
Duchess of Edinburgh, had attended a Lord's Taverners Ball
at Grosvenor House, where there was a cricket match and an
all-star cabaret, on the evening of 30 April. When she visited
Lord's in mid-summer, she witnessed a masterclass from**

Roy Tattersall and Johnny Wardle, who shared 13 of the 14 wickets South Africa lost in the day. Spin bowling dominated, and nobody made many runs.

It had rained overnight and, after short new-ball bursts from Bedser and Brian Statham, it became clear to England, led by Freddie Brown, that spin was going to be the order of the day. Lancashire's Roy Tattersall, a pacy off-break bowler, and Yorkshire's fractious ex-coal miner Johnny Wardle, a left-arm spinner with every conceivable variation, soon had South Africa in disarray. Wardle took the first wicket – John Waite caught by Hutton for 25 – before Tattersall scythed through the middle order. Jackie McGlew was caught behind by Evans, Eric Rowan was brilliantly held by Ikin at short-leg for 24 – the highest score of the innings – and Nourse was caught slog-sweeping. Tattersall took his first five-wicket haul in Tests – but he didn't stop there. After Wardle pinned Clive van Ryneveld in front, Tattersall added Athol Rowan and Mann, both caught, before himself catching Chubb off Wardle. The two spinners had shared all 10 wickets, Tattersall claiming 7 for 52, which would remain his career-best figures. South Africa followed on, 196 behind, with Bedser and Statham again taking the new ball. Statham dismissed Eric Rowan, caught by Ikin for the second time that day. Tattersall had Waite caught, and bowled McGlew – thus dismissing him twice in the day – before Wardle had Nourse lbw. South Africa closed on 137 for 4, and though Jack Cheetham and George Fullerton shared an unbroken partnership of 79, they were still 59 short of making England bat again.

The third morning was dark and damp. Bedser and Statham opened the bowling and got the breakthroughs. Cheetham and Fullerton had extended their stand by 15 when Cheetham lost his middle stump to Statham. Fullerton soon followed him, lbw. Both had made half-centuries, but once they had gone, England's path was clear. Tattersall returned to dismiss van Ryneveld, Chubb and Mann for his second five-for, completing a 12-wicket match haul, the best of his Test career. South Africa had nosed in front, but not by much: England needed just 16 to level the series. To give the spectators their money's worth, a beer match was played in the afternoon.

So began England's fightback. They won the low-scoring third Test on a wet pitch at Manchester, with Bedser taking 12 wickets. Chubb took a career-best 6 for 51 for South Africa, but England prevailed by nine wickets when Hutton made 98 not out in the second innings, two short of scoring his 100th first-class hundred. The fourth Test was drawn after Eric Rowan made 236 out of South Africa's 538; Hutton and Peter May, on his Test debut, both scored centuries for England. England won the fifth Test at The Oval, another tense contest, thanks to Jim Laker's 10-wicket match. Hutton was given out obstructing the field during England's chase, trying to stop a ball he had just hit from bouncing onto the wicket, but preventing South Africa's wicketkeeper, Russell Endean, from taking a catch. Mann missed the game with an illness from which he died, aged 30, less than a year later.

Mankad's marathons

England v India at Lord's, 1952

India 235 (M. H. Mankad 72, V. S. Hazare 69; F. S. Trueman 4–72)
and 378 (M. H. Mankad 184; J. C. Laker 4–102, F. S. Trueman 4–110).
England 537 (L. Hutton 150, T. G. Evans 104, P. B. H. May 74, R. T.
Simpson 53; M. H. Mankad 5–196) **and 79 for 2. England won by
eight wickets.**

England went one-up in the four-Test series, winning by seven
wickets at Leeds. They were only held up in India's first innings by a
stand of 242 between captain Vijay Hazare, who made 89, and Vijay
Manjrekar, whose 133 was his maiden first-class century. The rest of
the innings accounted for just 51 runs, as Yorkshire's tearaway fast
bowler, Fred Trueman, and Laker shared seven wickets. England
made a steady reply, batting 165 overs for 334, a lead of 41. Tom
Graveney top-scored with 71, but the innings was given pep by
Evans's sprightly 66. India's off-spinner, Ghulam Ahmed, wheeled
away for 63 overs, collecting 5 for 100. India's second innings was
famously disastrous: they were 0 for 4, with Trueman dismissing
Pankaj Roy, Madhav Mantri and Manjrekar. This soon became
26 for 5, but Hazare and Dattu Phadkar put on 105 to avert total
humiliation. Even so, England's target of 125 was easily attained, for
the loss of three wickets.

India needed a hero in the second Test: step forward, Vinoo
Mankad. After deciding to bat, he hit a breezy 72 in an opening
stand of 106 with Roy, before being caught at short fine-leg off
Trueman. This was the beginning of a slide for India, who were
out for 235, despite Hazare's unbeaten 69 from No. 4; Trueman
took four wickets. England then began a masterclass of watchful
accumulation: they were only one down when they passed India's
total, with new captain Hutton making 150 in five hours and 18
minutes. Evans ambled to the wicket at the start of the third day
and came within two runs of scoring a century before lunch; after it,
he equalled his previous highest Test score of 105, facing 135 balls,

and helped England to inflate their advantage to 302. Mankad had sent down 73 overs of his slow left-armers, taking 5 for 196. India were soon 59 for 2, but they recovered by the close of the third day, when they were 137 for 2, Mankad scoring 86 of them.

Fourth day – 23 June

On her first visit to Lord's as sovereign, HM Queen Elizabeth witnessed an engrossing battle between England's bowling attack, spearheaded by the pace of Fred Trueman and the wiles of Jim Laker, and India's great all-rounder Vinoo Mankad. He carried his team almost single-handedly in this match, and his counter-attacking 184 threatened to undo England's plans. Even when he was dismissed – and after the rest of his team had swiftly followed – he took the new ball and bowled unchanged until the close, making England work to reach their target.

Mankad took an aggressive approach next day. Seeing off Laker but going after Trueman and leg-spinner Roly Jenkins, he advanced his score to an India-record 184 out of 270. He had batted for 283 minutes and taken India to within 32 of parity when Laker got through his defences with a yorker. Hazare, whose supporting role was characterised by all-out defence, was soon caught off Bedser for 49, made in just under six hours. England seized their moment. Laker winkled out Manjrekar, Phadkar and Mantri; Trueman, maintaining a good pace, got Polly Umrigar, Gulabrai Ramchand and Sadashiv Shinde. India had lost eight for 108, setting England 77 to win. They got 40 of them that evening, for the loss of Simpson.

An exhausted Mankad rubbed the ball on the ground to remove the shine and bowled throughout the England innings, sending down 24 wicketless overs costing 35 runs, for match figures of 97–36–231–5. But his all-round efforts – his 256 runs in the match came in over seven hours at the crease – counted for little. England crawled to their target in the 50th over, taking a 2–0 lead in the series.

England won the third Test at Old Trafford by an innings after Hutton had made another watchful century and Evans had enjoyed another spree of hitting (71 off 78 balls). Trueman took a career-best 8 for 31 as India capitulated for 58; Bedser and Tony Lock shared nine wickets in the follow-on. Mankad was a spent force, scoring 4 and 6, and sending down 28 comparatively ineffectual overs. No Indian managed more than Hemchandra Adhikari's second-innings 27, as they were bowled out twice on the third day.

Things started just as badly for them in the fourth Test at The Oval. England again batted first, with Hutton making 86 and David Sheppard completing his maiden Test hundred. England declared at 326, and bowled India out for 98 (Mankad scored 5), with Bedser and Trueman taking five wickets apiece. But rain prevented more play than it permitted, and India were spared another challenging follow-on by a fifth-day washout.

The taming of Compton and Edrich

Middlesex v Australians at Lord's, 1953

Middlesex 150 (R. R. Lindwall 4–40) **and 112 for 4** (H. P. H. Sharp 51). **Australia 416** (J. H. de Courcy 74, K. R. Miller 71, R. G. Archer 58*, R. Benaud 52; A. E. Moss 4–103). **Drawn.**

The Ashes series of 1953 may not look, on paper, especially exciting as a contest: the first four Tests were drawn, and England secured a tidy win at The Oval. But it was England's first victorious Ashes after a record 19 years without them, and the matches were gripping, swinging this way and that. And there were some thrilling talents in the Australian party, among them the scintillating Neil Harvey, who scored 2,040 first-class runs on the tour, including 10 centuries; inspirational captain Lindsay Hassett, who hit five hundreds, including two in the Tests; effervescent all-rounder Keith Miller, who averaged 51 with the bat and 22 with the ball; young leg-spinner Richie Benaud, who took 57 wickets; and the fast bowlers Ray Lindwall and Alan Davidson, who shared 135 victims. Lindwall, eight years Davidson's senior, had taken him under his wing. He was furious to see Davidson bowl a bouncer at an opposing No. 8. "You've just admitted he can bat better than you can bowl," Lindwall complained. "Get into the nets and learn how to bowl properly."

Australia had innings victories against Leicestershire, Yorkshire, Surrey, both Oxford and Cambridge universities, and a Minor Counties XI – and that was just in May. A series of draws set them up for the Tests, which yielded more of the same. By mid-July, in the break between the third and fourth Tests, they were unbeaten in 21 matches, winning 11. Having made a flying visit to The Hague to play the Netherlands, they came to a rainy Lord's, where Edrich, captaining Middlesex, won the toss and elected to bat. The weather prevented much play, and they were 71 for 1 at the close.

Second day – 20 July

This was the first time the Queen visited a non-international game. At last, she got to see Compton and Edrich bat, but not for long. Ray Lindwall, the great Australian fast bowler, was in his pomp, and Richie Benaud, the young leg-spinner, was skilful and accurate. Middlesex made only 150. The Australian captain Lindsay Hassett batted attractively and Keith Miller, the rumbustious all-rounder, hit a belligerent half-century by the close.

Lindwall was an out-and-out fast bowler, and with that came exhaustion. After watching footage of himself bowling, he was amazed to see how energetic he appeared: "I don't *look* tired," he exclaimed. He opened the bowling on the second day, and soon took the second Middlesex wicket. This brought Compton and Edrich together in the middle; the Queen would finally get to see the famous duo bat, having only watched them bowl during their golden season, six years earlier. She liked Compton, and Compton seemed not to be starstruck. "Denis could mix comfortably with kings and queens and the working man," Miller later recalled. "Everybody loved Compo." Rumours that admiration for Compton persuaded the Queen to support Arsenal, for whom he played football during the winter, were circulated by their midfielder Cesc Fabregas in 2007. Compton was awarded a CBE in 1958.

On this day, alas, he lasted mere minutes, falling lbw to Lindwall. Then on came the spinners: wrist-spinner Doug Ring and off-spinner Graeme Hole worked their way through the middle order, while Benaud was economical, though wicketless. Edrich battled hard, top-scoring with 49 out of 150, as Lindwall finished with 4 for 40. Hassett opened Australia's innings with some handsome shots, but three wickets fell – including his – before 100 was raised. Then came Miller. Hitting boldly, he proceeded to an aggressive half-century, and was 60 not out at the close.

There was only one day left and once Australia decided against setting Middlesex a competitive chase a draw was inevitable.

Australia batted on to 416, a lead of 266, giving their hosts only 39 overs to face late in the day; they settled for batting practice.

Australia had extended their unbeaten sequence to 28 games by the time they got to The Oval for the fifth Test, where they were undone by Laker and Lock. It was their only defeat of the tour; after losing the Ashes, they played eight more games, winning five. Benaud had endured a difficult tour, the seam of the English ball cutting his fingers painfully, but he signed off with a world-record 11 sixes in his 135 at Scarborough. He rated Hassett the best captain he played under. Hassett gave a gracious speech before returning home, having been given the epithet 'Happy Warrior'. Like Benaud, he became a commentator when his playing days ended, once wryly remarking in the press box, "I'm glad I wasn't up here when I was down there".

An Australian cricket festival

Adelaide, 1954

During the Queen's eight-week tour of Australia with Prince Philip, she visited 57 towns and cities, from Cairns in the north to Hobart in the south. They arrived in South Australia on Thursday 18 March and were met by the Premier, Tom Playford, who entertained them at Government House. On Friday morning, there was a Royal Progress through Adelaide, attended by 300,000 deliriously excited townsfolk. In the afternoon, the entourage went to the races at Morpettville, where a Queen's Cup was run, then visited the Adelaide Oval.

Don Bradman had been knighted in 1949, the only Australian cricketer to receive the honour. He was part of the welcoming party at the Oval, where a match was staged between the South Australian Cricket Association and the Country Cricket Association. The chairman of the latter was Vic Richardson, who played cricket and baseball for Australia, had represented South Australia in Australian rules football and golf, and had won the state title in tennis. He was, perhaps, Australia's greatest sportsman.

Bradman and Richardson meeting the Queen was a newsworthy occasion in itself – and eclipsed the cricket in terms of of column inches. "The cricket match was important only as a Royal entertainment," announced *The West Australian* of Perth. "Play was almost perfunctory, except when Royal eyes were watching it." Brisbane's *Courier-Mail* found something else to focus on. "A sharp particle of dust flew into the Queen's left eye but, although it must have been causing her pain, she carried on," it cooed admiringly.

For local reporter Mary Armitage, writing in *The Advertiser*, matters of aesthetics and taste were top billing. "The Queen wore the same grey faille coat that she wore for the Royal Progress and the Queen's Cup," she enthused. "Her little peacock green and anthracite great feather cap glowed brilliantly against the bright green turf. Lady Bradman wore an ink blue faille coat over floral silk and lilac pink chiffon swathed her pillbox straw hat. Mrs Victor Richardson's cream straw bonnet had a soft organza bowl which touched the shoulders of her teal blue suit. Her husband, who is president of the Country Cricket Association, sat next to the Duke."

Fazal keeps his end up

MCC v Pakistan at Lord's, 1954

MCC 307 for 7 declared (R. T. Simpson 126) **and 210 for 6 declared** (P. B. H. May 61, M. C. Cowdrey 60*). **Pakistan 310 for 4 declared** (Imtiaz Ahmed 96, Maqsood Ahmed 94, Alim-ud-Din 61) **and 85 for 6. Drawn.**

Pakistan were elevated to Test status in 1952, playing their first series, in India, that October. Though it ended in defeat, they won a Test at Lucknow; the batting of Hanif Mohammad, the bowling of Fazal Mahmood and the astute captaincy of Abdul Kardar – who had played for India in 1946 – came to widespread notice.

Pakistan's second assignment was a tour to the UK in 1954, with a match in Cairo en route, games against Scotland and Canada, and four Tests against England. They were utterly unfamiliar with the conditions. The weather was cold, the pitches were slow and most of the Pakistanis had only previously played on matting. But while they were inexperienced, they were also enthusiastic and eager to learn. Beginning their tour in May, the tourists beat Worcestershire and Oxford University and drew two other games before arriving at Lord's.

Hanif had scored twin fifties at Leicester; Fazal had taken 7 for 28 in Cairo, 11 wickets in Worcester, and 5 for 54 in 38 overs against Oxford. There was much anticipation ahead of their match with MCC, who selected four internationals: Trevor Bailey, Brian Close, May and Simpson. Also in the team was off-spinner Robin Marlar, then with Sussex after graduating from Cambridge, and Colin Cowdrey, yet to play for England but on his way to 1,000 runs in a season for the fourth year in succession.

First day – 22 May

The Queen attended the first day of the game. MCC, captained by Trevor Bailey, decided to bat and stayed at the wicket

the whole day, making 307 for 7. Fazal Mahmood was the pick of the Pakistani bowlers, sending down 42 of the 103.4 overs bowled, and taking 2 for 89, with 17 maidens. Reg Simpson was England's mainstay, scoring 126, while Peter May contributed an attractive 43.

Simpson's innings lasted 210 minutes; he put on 128 with his opening partner, Neville Rogers of Hampshire – by then nearing the end of his county career – and 78 with May. There was a Pakistani fightback in the afternoon, led by Fazal, whose figures of 42–17–89–2 represented a Herculean day's work. England slipped from 206 for 1 to 253 for 6, but captain Bailey and Middlesex's Don Bennett added 54 for the seventh wicket. England declared overnight.

Pakistan had the best of things on day two. Though Hanif went early, Alim-ul-Din and Imtiaz Ahmed put on 100, before Maqsood Ahmed joined Imtiaz in adding another 152. Both were out in the nineties: Imtiaz was caught off Bailey and Maqsood hit a return catch to Bennett. Pakistan declared as soon as they passed England's total. On the third day, MCC wanted to set up a run-chase, but slid to 46 for 3 before May and Cowdrey rescued them with half-centuries; Fazal again sent down more than a third of the overs, collecting 2 for 45. Bailey declared just before tea, setting Pakistan 208 from what turned out to be 50 overs, a tough proposition which became tougher when Marlar started picking up wickets. MCC were given an extra half-hour to try and bowl Pakistan out, but the visitors resisted manfully, finishing on 85 for 6.

The next four tour games were drawn, as was the first Test at Lord's, where the first three days were lost to rain. The Queen had been due to attend the opening day, June 10, so a reception for both teams was hastily arranged at Buckingham Palace two days later, the first time cricketers had been invited to meet the Queen there. Compton – an ever-present for England and Middlesex – met her for the fifth time. Receptions for touring teams would become a regular feature of the Palace calendar.

Pakistan were undefeated until their 16th match, when they met Yorkshire. They lost the second Test at Trent Bridge and drew the third at Old Trafford, and then went unbeaten throughout July and August. The visitors shared the Test series by winning the fourth Test at The Oval. No other team had won a Test on their first visit to England. Fazal was the hero, taking six wickets in each innings and preventing England scoring 168 to win, even though they had looked in control at 109 for 2.

Pakistan's third defeat was in their last game, against T. N. Pearce's XI at Scarborough. By that point, Fazal had finally run out of steam – he broke down at Canterbury in late August, having bowled 666 overs on the tour, taking 77 wickets at 17. In 1955, Fazal was the first Pakistani to be named one of *Wisden*'s Five Cricketers of the Year. Hanif had to wait until 1968 for the same honour.

Spin-off at The Oval

Surrey v South Africa at The Oval, 1955

South Africa 244 (R. A. McLean 151; P. J. Loader 4–46) **and 170** (J. C. Laker 5–56). **Surrey 140** (P. B. H. May 62; H. J. Tayfield 5–22) **and 192** (T. H. Clark 58; H. J. Tayfield 8–76). **South Africa won by 82 runs.**

Only Worcestershire had taken a match off the South Africans in their 10 tour games ahead of the first Test, off-spinner Martin Horton enjoying the day of his cricketing life with 9 for 56. The domination of spin presaged what was to come in the internationals: at Nottingham, Wardle, the slow left-armer, made South Africa follow on with figures of 32–23–24–4, then Frank Tyson's great pace blew them away with 6 for 28 in the second innings. But as June wore on, and pitches wore out, South Africa's own finger spinner, Hugh Tayfield, came into his own. His 5 for 80 in the second Test at Lord's gave the visitors a chance of chasing 183 to win, but this time it was Statham who foiled them, with a career-best 7 for 39.

South Africa hit back in the third Test at Manchester, three batters scoring centuries in their 521, in response to England's 284. Waite, the wicketkeeper, made 113 and Paul Winslow 108 – his only Test hundred – but it was McGlew who put the hardest yards in. Having made a pair at Lord's, he retired hurt with a hand injury when on 77, but resumed at the fall of the seventh wicket to complete his century. South Africa declared with a lead of 237, but resistance through May (117), Compton (71) and Cowdrey (50) left the visitors a target of 145, which they got – though not without jitters – with seven wickets down, and an over and a half left in the match.

There was a single tour match, at The Oval, between the third and fourth Tests. It was one of only two matches the Queen visited at Kennington, the other coming in 1991 (neither were Tests). Stuart Surridge's Surrey hosted the South Africans in what was clearly going to be a battle of the spinners: Laker versus Tayfield. Cheetham, the tourists' captain, was rested and Endean led the team; he did his first job well, winning the toss and choosing to bat. This was

South Africa's chance to get a big score before the pitch turned. But Surrey's seamers, Bedser and Loader, soon had them in trouble, sharing four wickets, and when Laker came on to pin Waite lbw, it was 115 for 5. Roy McLean, a burly hitter, saved the day with a counterattacking 151 out of 199 runs scored in the three and a half hours he was at the crease. Surrey, replying to 244, were 66 for 2 at the close; the following day was a Sunday, and thus a rest day.

Second day – 18 July

Peter May and Ken Barrington dug in for a time, but then Surrey collapsed against Hugh Tayfield, who finished with 5 for 22. South Africa had a lead of 104 but had to battle Jim Laker to set Surrey a target. He took 5 for 56, and restricted the visitors to 170, but with the pitch turning, a chase of 275 looked a tall order. Surrey had lost a wicket by the close.

May continued comfortably on the Monday morning, though he lost Bernie Constable at 83, and with Ken Barrington raised the score to 115 for 3. Endean brought Tayfield on, and everything changed. In the next three-quarters of an hour, Surrey were shot out for 140, Tayfield enjoying a spell of five wickets in eight overs. With a lead of 104, South Africa got to work setting their hosts a testing target, but the pitch was now taking appreciable spin, and Laker returned figures of 5 for 56, including the crucial wicket of McLean, for 15. By five o'clock, South Africa were all out: their 170 set Surrey 275 to win in a little over a day. Micky Stewart was out hit wicket before stumps, but 34 for 1 was a good start, especially with May and Barrington to come.

The pair were at the wicket by lunch on the final day, and Surrey still seemed in with a chance at 139 for 3. It was a different story in the afternoon. Tayfield ran through his variations as the ball bounced and turned, and once he had dismissed May (43) it was a procession. He took 8 for 76, ending with match figures of 13 for 98.

Buoyed by their victory, and with Tayfield now in full flight, South Africa levelled the Test series at Leeds, despite having been 98 for 7 on the first day. They managed to restrict England's lead to

20, before McGlew and Endean scored centuries in a total of 500. Needing 481 to win, England had no chance, especially against Tayfield, who picked up 5 for 94 – nine wickets in the match.

The fifth Test, at The Oval, made for a thrilling decider. England took a first-innings lead of 39, then May stuck it out for a five-hour unbeaten 89, as Tayfield wheeled away for figures of 53.4–29–60–5. South Africa needed 244 to claim the series, but in the fourth innings, against Laker and Lock, it was all but impossible, especially when Headley Keith, Endean and McLean made ducks. McGlew hung around 108 minutes for 19, but when Lock trapped him lbw it was 59 for 5, and the jig was up. Surrey's spin pairing had combined figures of 9 for 118, and England took the series.

Benaud and Miller take the lead

England v Australia at Lord's, 1956

Australia 285 (C. C. McDonald 78, J. W. Burke 65) **and 257** (R. Benaud 97; F. S. Trueman 5–90, T. E. Bailey 4–64). **England 171** (P. B. H. May 63; K. R. Miller 5–72) **and 186** (P. B. H. May 53; K. R. Miller 5–80, R. G. Archer 4–71). **Australia won by 185 runs.**

Australia's campaign to win back the Ashes, after another England win in 1954/55, began with 11 tour matches, of which they lost only one – against Surrey in May, for whom Laker took 10 for 88 in the first innings, a foreshadowing of the summer to come. The first Test at Nottingham was a rainy affair but there was enough play to establish Laker and Lock as the main threat to the Australians. England's new opener, Peter Richardson, made 81 and 73; Cowdrey partnered him, scoring 25 and 81. But it was the spin pairing who made the headlines, posing difficult questions on a wet pitch. The match was drawn, and a confident England headed south.

What confronted England at Lord's was a fast, true pitch offering good carry for the seamers; it more or less nullified the impact of the spinners. Lock had been taken ill and went to hospital, so Wardle stepped in to partner Laker, but they only managed four wickets between them in the match. Batting first, Australia made a good start when Colin McDonald and Jim Burke opened with 137, both scoring half-centuries. Bailey dismissed McDonald and Harvey, and from then on wickets fell at regular intervals.

It took Australia 146 overs to assemble a competitive 285, but they were hamstrung: Lindwall and Davidson had both been both injured in the first Test and they soon lost the services of replacement opening bowler Pat Crawford, who pulled a thigh muscle in his fifth over. It fell to Miller to take the lead again. Bowling lengthy spells, and swinging the ball both ways, he took 5 for 72; only May, with a handsome 63, and Bailey, dead-batting for 32, resisted for any length of time. Australia found themselves batting again, with a lead of 104, halfway through the third day. Trueman gave it everything, and by the close he had reduced the visitors to 115 for 6.

Fourth day – 25 June

Australia were 229 ahead, with four second-innings wickets in hand. Richie Benaud went for broke, taking on England's stellar attack of Brian Statham, Fred Trueman, Trevor Bailey, Jim Laker and Johnny Wardle, scoring 97 from 140 balls. His enterprise set England 372, and they opted to bat out time, keeping Benaud's leg-spin at bay, but struggling against Keith Miller, who took a 10-wicket match haul.

On the fourth morning, Benaud went on the offensive. He tore into the bowling, hitting 14 fours and a six, making 97 out of a seventh-wicket stand of 117 with Ken Mackay, who batted three and a half hours for 31. Only when Trueman took the new ball did Benaud make a mistake: trying to reach his hundred with a boundary, he top edged a catch behind. His dismissal completed Trueman's five-wicket haul but England's hopes of victory were exhausted. Their eventual target was 372; Richardson and Cowdrey made it to tea unscathed. In the evening session, the hosts batted with extreme caution, allowing Australia to set attacking fields. Peter Burge was posted at short-leg, a mere six feet from the bat. A siege was established, and England lost Richardson and Graveney before the close, both caught behind.

There was no chance of England scoring 300 to win on the final day, and they attempted to bat their way to a draw. Willie Watson missed a Miller full toss, Cowdrey fell lbw to Benaud, and Bailey went just before lunch. May and Evans were the last line of defence; May asked Ian Johnson, Australia's captain, to move Burge a little further from the bat, but it made no difference. Well supported by Ron Archer's four scalps, Miller took another five-wicket haul, and the match was won shortly before three o'clock. At 36 years of age, Miller had match figures of 10 for 152, in more than 70 overs. A fortnight later, he captained the tourists at Southampton, and was invited to dinner by Lord Mountbatten, who lived nearby. He sat next to HRH Princess Margaret, and later described "the bluest eyes I have ever seen". There was speculation of a romance. "No gentleman ever discusses any relationship with a lady," was Miller's response.

Chastened by seam, England knew what they had to do in the third and fourth Tests. They conjured up spin-friendly tracks at Leeds, where Laker and Lock shared 18 wickets, and Manchester, where they took all 20. Laker, of course, took 19 of them. They were well on their way in the fifth Test at The Oval, only for rain to end the contest with England five wickets from victory.

A county bun fight

Guildford, 1957

The Queen was at Windsor Castle when the 1957 Lord's Test began. West Indies were in town, but the Test clashed with the Royal Ascot races, and if there was one sporting event the Queen was guaranteed not to miss, it was Ascot. She liked cricket – but she adored racing. She was scheduled to return to London to watch day four – but England had won it by then. Instead, she held a reception for the West Indies team, just as she had done for the Pakistanis three years earlier. Here she met some of the greats of the age: the three Ws, Clyde Walcott, Everton Weekes and Frank Worrell; the famous spin pairing, Sonny Ramadhin and Alf Valentine; the up-and-coming batter, Rohan Kanhai, who had made his Test debut at Birmingham; fast bowler Wes Hall, who was still waiting to make his debut; the greatest all-rounder of the modern era, Garfield Sobers.

Four days later, on 28 June, the Queen visited Guildford, and it was decided that she would have tea with the mayor on the third afternoon of Surrey's County Championship match against Hampshire. But Surrey, and May in particular, had other plans. Bedser and Loader had blown Hampshire away for 66. Rather than bat on and guarantee play on day three, May declared with a lead of 181, and Hampshire were rolled for a second time in two days. Once again, the Queen arrived a day late, but the teams agreed to play a one-innings "bun-fight" match, and a huge crowd turned up to watch. This was the sixth time the Queen had met May, now England's captain as well as Surrey's, and they bantered like old friends. "This is the second time you have let me down," she told him, with mock indignation. "It's us who've let you down," replied Colin Ingleby-Mackenzie, the Hampshire captain. She enjoyed the scratch game nonetheless. "Cricket in this sort of surroundings is much more fun than sitting in a stuffy box at Lord's," she told the mayor. "Charles is learning to play cricket, but the easy way. I think it's much better than taking the game too seriously, too young."

May in March, rain in June

London, 1958

By 1958, Peter May had become a favourite of the Queen. The England team had no overseas commitments in 1957/58, so the England and Surrey captain was invited to Sunday lunch at Buckingham Palace on 6 March. The guests were a disparate bunch. John Simon, 2nd Viscount Simon, was the managing director of P&O Ferries, and chairman of the Port of London Authority; Sir George Edwards was an aircraft designer for Vickers Armstrongs, who led the British side of the Concorde project; Charles Orr-Ewing, MP for Hendon North, had worked on the first mass-produced television set, and was now in the Air Ministry; Noel Annan, a politics fellow, was provost of King's College, Cambridge; Sir Frederick Bishop was the principle private secretary to the prime minister, Harold Macmillan; Edward Davies was the general manager of the Press Association. How May fitted into that group is anybody's guess.

May let the Queen down a third time. Once again, she was at Royal Ascot during the first three days of the 1958 Lord's Test against New Zealand, and by the time she returned to London to watch the fourth, England had won. They had already emphatically won the first Test and at Lord's they needed only 269 to win by an innings: New Zealand were bowled out for 47 on the second day, and 74 on the third. On a rain-affected pitch, Laker and Lock shared 14 wickets for 66 runs. For the third time, the touring party were entertained at the Palace, led by John Reid, who may only have scored 147 runs and taken six wickets across the five Tests, but captained with pride and aplomb despite the 4–0 series defeat.

Typhoon season in St John's Wood

MCC v India at Lord's, 1959

MCC 374 for 4 declared (C. A. Milton 104, E. R. Dexter 100*, M. J. K. Smith 82,) **and 120 for 1 declared** (M. J. K. Smith 64*). **India 211** (C. G. Borde 88, P. R. Umrigar 82; A. E. Moss 5–41, F. H. Tyson 4–44) **and 136** (R. Illingworth 5–34). **MCC won by 147 runs.**

In anticipation of her early summer trip to Canada, which kept her from the Lord's Test, the Queen kept her cricket watching to late spring in 1959. On 9 May, she was given a tour of Wellington College in Berkshire, and briefly watched a school match. The main event of the season, though, was the visit of the Indians. England had won the first four Tests against New Zealand the previous year, only to be denied their first whitewash by rain at The Oval. They had high hopes of going one better this time. In preparation, India scheduled three friendlies and nine first-class matches before the first Test – but they beat only the Club Cricket Conference and Cambridge University, and lost to Glamorgan. They faced MCC at Lord's two weeks ahead of the first Test and were confronted with a strong eleven: seven had already played Tests and three would later do so; only Doug Slade, a left-arm spinner for Worcestershire, never got the call.

India won the toss and put MCC in, wary of facing the rapid Tyson after they'd been dismissed for 112 in their first innings against Glamorgan, and 188 against Essex. Arthur Milton, having scored a hundred on debut against New Zealand the previous July, made a confident start in a century opening stand and went on to make 104. Mike Smith, another of the 1958 intake, struck 82 and a third, Ted Dexter, took the game away from the Indians. His unbeaten 100 came in two hours after tea and set up a declaration on 374. Tyson let a few rockets fly but India survived until the close. The second day was dominated by the hosts. Tyson soon had

India 31 for 3, which brought together Umrigar – who had scored 252 against Cambridge, the highest score yet made by an Indian tourist in England – and Chandu Borde. They painstakingly put on a partnership of 159, which occupied most of the day, but when they were eventually parted, Tyson and Alan Moss cleaned up the rest. The collapse was seven for 21, including four ducks. It was a sorry procession. MCC had a lead of 163 but decided not to enforce the follow-on. The Queen was not due until the afternoon of the following day, and perhaps captain Doug Insole was worried India wouldn't last that long. He would have been right to worry.

Third day – 26 May

It was touch and go whether the Queen would see any play at Lord's – not because of the weather, but because MCC were in total control of the match, and India in disarray. The hosts managed to eke out the game to coincide with the Queen's afternoon visit, declining the opportunity to enforce the follow-on and playing out a couple of hours until she arrived. Then she saw, for the first time, the 'Typhoon' Frank Tyson, who sent down 11 rapid overs. And it was her first glimpse of Ray Illingworth, soon to be an England mainstay – and indeed captain – who took 5 for 34. India were nine down, desperately clinging on, when the players lined up to meet the Queen at tea.

MCC began the third and final day on 29 for 1 and seemed resolved to bat until play was guaranteed for the later arrival of the Queen. Smith and Geoff Pullar hung around, somewhat ponderously adding an unbeaten 101 for the second wicket, before it seemed safe to make a declaration on 120, setting India an impossible 284, but allowing just enough time to bowl them out. This time there was no backs-to-the-wall defiance. Tyson and Moss were in their element again, but the worst damage was done by Ray Illingworth, who collected 5 for 34 with his off-breaks. Bapu Nadkarni held out longest, for 36. Only a last-wicket partnership of 20 saved India from the ignominy of meeting the Queen after the match had concluded; as it was, they were nine down when they lined up to be presented to her majesty during the tea interval. Only 500 spectators stuck around that long. At least it was a novelty for most of the Indians – only Roy and Umrigar had met the Queen before.

India lost the first Test at Trent Bridge by an innings, with May scoring 106 and Statham and Trueman sharing 13 wickets. They managed a third win of the tour, at Northampton, but lost to the Minor Counties. Nari Contractor made a heroic 81 in the second Test at Lord's, but India came unstuck against leg-spinner Tommy Greenhough, who took 5 for 35. Another innings defeat came in the third Test at Leeds, with Cowdrey making 160. Then Pullar and Smith scored centuries as England won the fourth Test at Old Trafford before the whitewash was completed with another Statham and Trueman show at The Oval. India beat Middlesex, Glamorgan and Kent, but lost to Nottinghamshire, Gloucestershire, and T. N. Pearce's XI at Scarborough, which comprised a full complement of past or future international players.

The throwing controversy

England v South Africa at Lord's, 1960

England 362 for 8 declared (M. J. K. Smith 99, R. Subba Row 90,
E. R. Dexter 56, P. M. Walker 52; G. M. Griffin 4–87). **South Africa 152**
(J. B. Statham 6–63; A. E. Moss 4–35) **and 137** (J. B. Statham 5–34).
England won by an innings and 73 runs.

Time was running out for South Africa. Since the war, the UK had, to
some extent, turned a blind eye to Apartheid, which had been steadily
gathering pace since 1948. A significant sea change in South African
sport came with the first specific participation restrictions in 1956.
International anti-Apartheid actions began to germinate; in the UK,
the first substantial boycott movement gained momentum in 1959.
But 1960 was arguably the most shocking, turbulent year yet. The
Sharpeville massacre of 21 March sharply focused the world's attention,
and when South Africa – as was their custom – sent an all-white team
to England that summer, there were protests. In the eyes of many, the
MCC had invited the wrong organisation on tour. "The South African
Cricket Association is run on the basis of a colour bar, and all who
wish to join must be of pure white descent," read a leaflet from the
Anti-Apartheid Committee. "There is a multi-racial Association, but this
is not recognised as the official body by the MCC. Please remember
that a part of your admission money will go to the funds of the SACA."

MCC gave the South African board the option of cancelling, but
they decided to come, and there were minor demonstrations outside
every ground they played at. A huge on-field controversy unfolded,
too. Its seeds were sown when MCC played South Africa at Lord's in
May: umpires John Langridge and Frank Lee no-balled the visiting
fast bowler, Geoff Griffin, for throwing. Then at Nottingham, a
week later, he was called eight times. Griffin visited Alf Gover, the
renowned coach at Spencer CC in south London, for three days of
remedial training. He made his international debut in the first Test
at Edgbaston, which England won by 100 runs. But in a tour match
at Southampton, he was no-balled again.

And so to Lord's, where England, captained by Cowdrey, chose to bat. The opening day was rainy, but Dexter made an attractive 56, and Raman Subba Row began a five-hour innings of 90, which continued into day two. Over both days, Lee no-balled Griffin for throwing 11 times. Subba Row found a willing – and equally adhesive – ally in Smith, who had reached 99 when he was caught behind from the last ball of Griffin's 29th over. Then, with the first and second balls of his 30th – the last over of the day – Griffin bowled Peter Walker and Trueman, completing the first hat-trick in a Test at Lord's. England declared overnight. On the third day, South Africa were out for 152, courtesy of a supreme spell of fast bowling by Statham, who claimed 6 for 63. The visitors followed on 210 behind, and there was just enough time before a huge thunderstorm for Statham to dismiss McGlew for the second time in the day.

Fourth day – June 27

Brian Statham took 11 for 97, the best figures of his international career, and won the Test for England at half past two. But the Queen had not yet arrived, so an exhibition match was hastily staged. Matters became serious when Geoff Griffin was repeatedly no-balled for throwing, just as he had been in the Test.

After the customary Sunday rest day, South Africa resumed their struggle – one wicket down, and still 176 short of making England bat again. The pitch was ideal for seam; England only bowled one over of spin in the match. A crowd of 27,000 awaited the wickets and kept an eye out for the Queen, who was due at tea. The match did not get that far. Statham bowled for three hours with barely a break, taking 5 for 34 to give him 11 wickets in the match. There was no change of the Royal plans this year; the Queen was already on her way, so the teams staged a light-hearted exhibition match for her benefit. At least, it should have been light-hearted, but there was a sting in the tail. Griffin was brought on to bowl, captain McGlew judiciously choosing umpire Syd Buller's end this time. But Buller no-balled Griffin four times out of five. McGlew intervened and instructed Griffin to switch to underarm – legal in those days – only for Buller to call another no-ball, because the batter had not been informed of the change. The Queen arrived just as this was happening.

England won the third Test at Trent Bridge, with Trueman taking nine wickets, and the fourth at Old Trafford was drawn after rain washed out the first two days. South Africa gained a big first-innings lead in the final match of the series at The Oval but were denied a consolation victory by Pullar and Cowdrey, who both made centuries in an opening stand of 290, which forced a draw. Griffin did not bowl again on the tour after the trauma of Lord's and never played another match for South Africa. The Queen side-stepped the South Africans' visit in 1965, as opposition to Apartheid became impossible to ignore. She would not meet another South African cricket side for 34 years.

Davidson does the damage

England v Australia at Lord's, 1961

England 206 (A. K. Davidson 5–42) and 202 (K. F. Barrington 66; G. D. McKenzie 5–37). Australia 340 (W. M. Lawry 130, K. D. Mackay 54; F. S. Trueman 4–118) and 71 for 5. Australia won by five wickets.

There was growing concern about first-class cricket by the early sixties. Attendances were diminishing rapidly in the face of increasingly boring, one-sided matches – and Test cricket was no exception. England had hardly been stretched in the four summers since the Australians last visited in 1956. But there was a new sense of excitement around the Australia team of 1961. They were holders of the Ashes, having regained them under Benaud's captaincy in 1958/59, and had played exciting cricket the winter before they came to England, beginning with the tied Test at Brisbane in December 1960. Benaud's men were expected to be entertaining and strong – and they did not disappoint. They beat Lancashire, Surrey and Cambridge University in May, before bowling England out for 195 in the first Test at Edgbaston, and racking up 516 in reply, before rain forced a draw.

Benaud's shoulder was injured ahead of the second Test at Lord's, so Harvey captained Australia for the only time. MCC, exasperated after the Queen had missed play in all three Lord's Tests she was scheduled to attend since the previous Ashes, arranged for her to visit on the first day. All her previous visits to Tests at headquarters, as sovereign, had been on the fourth day: the Monday after the rest day. She returned to this pattern the following year.

First day – 22 June

Alan Davidson launched a spell of fire and fury at England. Despite boasting a line-up including Ted Dexter, Colin Cowdrey, Peter May and Ken Barrington, the hosts were overwhelmed as the ball flew sharply off a length. Davidson's

5 for 42 reduced the hosts to 167 for 9 before last pair Fred Trueman and Brian Statham added 39, then took a wicket apiece before the close.

The Queen was now well acquainted with the English team; she had already met all of the Lord's XI save for Tony Lock. England had a tough day. By 1961, there was much discussion around a ridge developing on the Lord's square, and the pitch certainly seemed uneven; the ball flew off a length at the Nursery End, and several batters were battered and bruised by the fast bowlers. England, more through luck than judgement, made it through most of the first session with only one wicket down: Pullar, bowled by Davidson for 11. He had been put down by Burge at gully; Bill Lawry reprieved Ted Dexter at short-leg, and Wally Grout dropped Subba Row behind the wicket. But, just before lunch, both went with the score on 87. May, playing his first Test for 16 months, was cheered to the crease – having just met the Queen for the seventh time – but he soon gloved a Davidson lifter to Grout. Captain Cowdrey fell in similar fashion to debutant Graham McKenzie. Davidson bowled with pace and aggression to finish with 5 for 42; England were 167 for 9 before Trueman and Statham added 39. They then tore in with the new ball, dismissing McDonald and Bobby Simpson before stumps.

Lawry had only made his debut the previous game, scoring a steady 57 before chasing a very wide ball from Illingworth. He did not make the same mistake this time, holding out for more than six hours for 130. Australia had been in a spot of trouble at 88 for 4, but Lawry found a tenacious partner in Burge, with whom he added 95. Lawry was finally dismissed after tea on the second day, seventh out with the lead 32. Grout followed immediately, but the last two wickets added 102. Facing a deficit of 334, England again struggled against pace. Pullar hung around, and Barrington batted over three hours for 66, but the hosts could only manage to set a target of 69. McKenzie finished with figures of 29–13–37–5 as the last four fell for 11. But Trueman and Statham gave it everything – the bounce was more unpredictable than ever – and reduced Australia to 19 for 4 before Burge and Simpson saw their team home. As soon as the match was over, MCC called in the pitch inspectors, who found several corrugations in the surface; the authorities promised to have it fixed in time for next year's Test.

The series came alive at Leeds, where the third Test became known as "Trueman's Match". Benaud returned to lead Australia, and May took back the England captaincy from Cowdrey; the pitch was again the villain. Some balls grubbed, and others stopped in the surface. It was a bowler's paradise. Trueman reduced Australia's first innings from 187 for 2 to 237 all out, producing a spell of 5 for 16. Davidson replied with 5 for 63, but England forged a lead of 62. Australia had erased the deficit and were 102 for 3 when Trueman struck again: this time he took five for nothing in 24 balls, as Australia lost seven for 18, and England knocked off their target of 59 with ease. Another Lawry century set England 256 to win the fourth Test at Old Trafford, but Benaud's 6 for 70 made it Australia's game. The tourists retained the Ashes when the fifth Test at The Oval was drawn.

The Pakistanis at the Palace again

London, 1962

Racing got in the way again in 1962, when – perhaps now predictably – the Lord's Test clashed with the Ascot meeting. The Queen remained at Windsor Castle until the Test was over; had the match continued to the fourth day, she would likely have visited Lord's, but since it finished in three, the Pakistani touring team were invited to Buckingham Palace, as they had been eight years earlier. They had a tough time of things against England, now led by Dexter. Despite brave centuries from Javed Burki and Nasim-ul-Ghani at Lord's, and Mushtaq Mohammad at Nottingham, they went down 4–0, and would probably have been whitewashed but for rain at Trent Bridge. Fazal Mahmood did battle gamely, but was not the force of old. There were hundreds in abundance for England, including three for Peter Parfitt.

A last-ball finish

England v West Indies at Lord's, 1963

West Indies 301 (R. B. Kanhai 73, J. S. Solomon 56; F. S. Trueman 6–100) **and 229** (B. F. Butcher 133; F. S. Trueman 4–52, D. Shackleton 4–72). **England 297** (K. F. Barrington 80, E. R. Dexter 70, F. J. Titmus 52; C. C. Griffith 5–91) **and 228 for 9** (D. B. Close 70, K. F. Barrington 60; W. W. Hall 4–93). **Drawn.**

The Queen witnessed one of the greatest Tests ever played at Lord's when England hosted the West Indies in 1963. She had received many of the era's great West Indians at the Palace in 1957; now she got to see them in action. Two of the three Ws had retired, as had Ramadhin and Valentine, but Worrell was back – now as captain – as were Kanhai and Sobers. Hall now had an equally fearsome new-ball partner in Charlie Griffith. They had been highly successful in the lead up to the Test series, winning seven games and losing only to L. C. Stevens' XI and Yorkshire. And in the first Test, on a turning pitch at Manchester, West Indies reigned supreme: Conrad Hunte scored 182, and England lost by an innings, with off-spinner Lance Gibbs taking 11 for 157 in the match.

West Indies batted first again at Lord's, scoring 301 against the relentless Trueman and Derek Shackleton, who bowled 94.2 overs between them, for nine wickets. On the second day, John Edrich was out first ball, and England were soon 20 for 2. Dexter then launched into a captain's innings of powerful drives and hooks, reaching his half-century in less than an hour, and finishing with 70 off 73 balls; it is still spoken about as one of the great innings at Lord's. Barrington made a fluent 80, and Fred Titmus chipped in with an unbeaten 52, as England reached 297; Griffith bowled his heart out, claiming 5 for 91. The game was in the balance when West Indies lost half their wickets for 104, but Worrell stopped the rot with sound defence, allowing Basil Butcher to go for his shots. And go for them he certainly did. The pair put on 110 by the end of day three – Butcher 129 not out – and had a lead of 218 going into the rest day.

Fourth day – 24 June

Ferocious fast bowling from Fred Trueman, who completed another five-wicket haul, shot out West Indies' remaining five wickets for 15. England began a chase of 234, but Wes Hall wasn't to be outdone by Trueman, and quickly dismissed Micky Stewart and John Edrich; Lance Gibbs got rid of Ted Dexter. A rescue mission was begun by Ken Barrington and Colin Cowdrey, who resisted manfully until Hall broke Cowdrey's wrist. Bad light stopped play with England 116 for 3, needing 118 more for victory.

West Indies lasted just six more overs on the Monday morning. Trueman burst through the tail, ending with 5 for 52 (11 for 152 in the match) as the last five wickets went for 15. Butcher added only four to his overnight score. England thus needed 234 to win. Things didn't look good for the hosts when Hall removed Stewart and Edrich, and Gibbs bowled Dexter, leaving England 31 for 3 before lunch. Barrington and Cowdrey fought back in the afternoon session, taking the score to 72, when a lifter from Hall broke Cowdrey's wrist. Barrington hit Gibbs for a couple of sixes, and bad light stopped play with England still needing 118.

It wasn't bright enough to play until well after two o'clock on the final afternoon; England managed only 18 in the first hour, Barrington adding five before edging a ball from Griffith. Jim Parks hit out until Griffith pinned him in front – 158 for 5, with 76 still to get. Then came what seemed a decisive stand: Close and Titmus took the score to 203, the former taking charge with his first Test half-century. But Hall got Titmus and Trueman with successive balls, and Griffith removed Close with 15 required. There were only 19 minutes left on the clock: all results were possible. Hall, running on fumes, steamed in for his 40th and final over with England needing eight to win. After a dot ball, Shackleton found a single, then David Allen did likewise, but Shackleton was run out at the bowler's end, attempting another quick run from the fourth ball. Out to the middle strode Cowdrey, his arm in plaster, to take his position at the non-striker's end. Allen, needing a boundary, decided not to risk it, and blocked the final deliveries of a nail-biting draw.

England drew level in the third Test at Edgbaston, setting West Indies 309 to win and brushing them aside for 91; Trueman took 7 for 44 to finish with 12 wickets in the match. West Indies retook the lead in the fourth Test at Headingley, Sobers making 102 and 52, and Griffith claiming 6 for 36 in England's first innings. Then, at The Oval, Griffith took 6 for 71 before Conrad Hunte (80 and 108 not out) sealed a West Indian chase of 253 – and the series.

Edrich's endurance

England v Australia at Lord's, 1964

Australia 176 (T. R. Veivers 54; F. S. Trueman 5–48) **and 168 for 4**
(P. J. P. Burge 59). **England 246** (J. H. Edrich 120; G. E. Corling 4–60).
Drawn.

By 1964, Australia had won three Ashes in a row, but by the time
they returned to England, they were a team in transition. Benaud,
Davidson and Harvey had called time on their international careers,
and it was a young – and comparatively weak – squad that set off
round the counties in April. But by the time they came to Nottingham
for the first Test, they were unbeaten in 11 matches, having won
five; Simpson and Lawry had become a redoubtable opening pair,
and a very strong MCC batting line-up had been turned over twice
by McKenzie and Grahame Corling.

The latter made his Test debut at Trent Bridge, as did a 23-year-
old from Yorkshire by the name of Geoffrey Boycott. He took 16
balls to get off the mark after England chose to bat, eventually
doing so with a four, and top-scored with 48 as England crawled to
216 for 8 between heavy showers on the first two days. The third
was washed out entirely, which more or less ended any chance of
a result, but England declared and hoped for a lucky break. They
prospered in damp conditions on day four, dismissing Australia for
168, and extended their lead to 119 without losing a wicket by the
close (Boycott had broken a finger while fielding and was ruled
out for a month). England were short of time to achieve a positive
result and McKenzie took 5 for 53 as they pushed for runs; their
declaration left Australia 242 to win in a little over three hours. Rain
had the final say, though, ending the match in the 10th over.

England picked two spinners for the second Test at Lord's,
Norman Gifford earning his first cap to join forces with Titmus.
There was uncertainty about how the relaid Lord's pitch would play,
so England chose to field. But, once again, the weather intervened,
and no play was possible until the third day. When the match finally

began, Australia found Trueman a handful: he took his fifth five-wicket haul at Lord's; it was the 17th – and last – of his career. Tom Veivers mounted a recovery of sorts after Australia slid to 88 for 6, but a total of 176 was barely competitive. England were 26 for the loss of Dexter – the captain acting as makeshift opener in Boycott's absence – by the close. The Sunday was a rest day.

Fourth day – 22 June

Of all the days of Test cricket the Queen attended, the Monday at Lord's in 1964 was among the most attritional. Australia's seamers bowled tirelessly for most of the day: Graham McKenzie taking key wickets in the morning, and Grahame Corling working through the lower order in the afternoon. England's rock was John Edrich, who batted five hours and 17 minutes for 120 – his maiden Test hundred, in his first Ashes appearance. The hosts' lead was 70, and Australia reached 49 for 1 by stumps.

Cowdrey and Barrington were out to McKenzie early in the day, leaving England 42 for 3, but Parfitt hung around for nearly an hour, adding 41 with Edrich. When he was lbw to Corling for 20, Phil Sharpe took up the fight, and proved Edrich's most durable partner, sharing a fifth-wicket stand of 55. Then came Parks, who added 32 with Edrich in less than half an hour, and Titmus, who saw England past Australia, and Edrich to his century. It had been a mostly watchful, doughty innings, punctuated by tension-relieving shots, including nine fours and two sixes. Corling took 4 for 60, his best Test figures – this would be his only series – as he went through the tail. Gifford had dismissed Lawry by the end of play but there was no twist on the final day. Australia got their feet under the table, scoring 168 for 4 by mid-afternoon, at which point the rain returned to chalk up another draw.

The series was all square heading into the third Test at Leeds, though Australia had added victories against the Minor Counties and Northamptonshire and were still unbeaten on the tour. The Test would be remembered for a heroic innings by Burge, who not only saved Australia from a substantial first-innings deficit, but earned them a match-winning lead. England made 268, with Dexter and Parks scoring half-centuries, and Neil Hawke taking 5 for 75. Australia reached 124 for 1, then collapsed after Lawry was run out for 78. With the spinners wheeling away at one end, and Trueman steaming in from the other, they had slipped to 178 for 7 when Burge launched into his counter-attacking, match-stealing 160, adding 105 with Hawke and 89 with Grout, and building a decisive lead of 121. England were bowled out for 229.

Having won by three wickets, Australia knew a draw in the fourth Test at Old Trafford would secure the Ashes, so Simpson decided to bat – and bat long. After opening with 201 alongside Lawry, he batted over 12 hours for 311. Australia made 656, and England replied with 611, Barrington completing his own marathon (256 in 11 and a half hours) as the hosts lasted 293 overs, 93 of which were bowled by Veivers. Australia, their mission complete, switched off, losing to Glamorgan and Warwickshire before drawing the fifth Test at The Oval – with the assistance of yet more rain.

Without the banished Barrington

England v New Zealand at Lord's, 1965

New Zealand 175 (V. Pollard 55, B. R. Taylor 51; F. E. Rumsey 4–25) **and 347** (B. W. Sinclair 72, G. T. Dowling 66, V. Pollard 55). **England 307** (M. C. Cowdrey 119, E. R. Dexter 62; R. O. Collinge 4–82) **and 218 for 3** (E. R. Dexter 80*, G. Boycott 76). **England won by seven wickets.**

At last, the English cricket authorities alighted upon a solution to the long, one-sided international seasons which had blighted the late 1950s and early 1960s. Taking their lead from the experimental, infamous summer of 1912 – experimental because it involved a three-team triangular series, infamous because it rained more or less constantly – they decided to invite New Zealand from April until July, and South Africa from June until September. Each played three Tests, thus sparing the public a full five-match series of mismatches.

England, now captained by Smith, were much stronger than New Zealand. In the first Test at Birmingham, Barrington's cautious century, with support from Cowdrey, carried England to 300 for 3 before a bowling fightback restricted them to 435. New Zealand were tumbled by Titmus and followed on 319 behind. After falling to 145 for 4, they managed to dig in; seven men passed 40 but no one exceeded Vic Pollard's unbeaten 81. England needed 95 and knocked off the runs with only one wicket lost. It was a cheerless contest, played in cold weather; only about 21,000 people attended in total, and just 107 turned up to watch England's fifth-day chase.

The England selectors felt something needed to be done to encourage people to come to Lord's for the second Test. They took the brave and controversial decision to omit Barrington, ostensibly as punishment for taking over seven hours to compile 137 at Edgbaston. They brought in Parfitt in his place and gave a debut to the young

Sussex tearaway quick, John Snow. New Zealand chose to bat and were 28 for 4 within an hour; Somerset's Fred Rumsey, sharing the new ball with Trueman, took all four. Snow was then brought on for his first bowl, and added two wickets of his own. From 62 for 6, the visitors rebuilt through a stand of 92 between Pollard and Bruce Taylor. When Taylor departed, Trueman and Taylor quickly wrapped up the innings for 175. Dick Motz, the fastest bowler in the New Zealand side, dismissed both England's openers by the close but they batted throughout the second day, led by Cowdrey's attractive 119; no bowler troubled him as much as his bad back. New Zealand persevered, and from 271 for 4, England were all out for 307 – a lead of 132. On day three, New Zealand closed the deficit for the loss of only Bev Congdon and, as at Birmingham, they proved much more tenacious second time around. They were 261 for 7 going into the rest day: 129 ahead, and with Pollard still there.

Fourth day – 21 June

It rained until the Queen arrived in mid-afternoon. New Zealand managed to add 86 before Bob Barber's leg-spin finished off the innings; Vic Pollard made 55 for the second time in the Test. England's target was 216; Geoff Boycott had knocked off 64 with Barber by the close.

Play did not begin on the Monday until quarter past two, owing to rain. The pitch was getting better all the time, and Pollard progressed sedately to his second 55 of the match. He batted for well over four hours; New Zealand had to try and push the game into five days to make England scrap for victory. Bob Barber dismantled the Kiwi tail with his leg-breaks, then padded up to begin England's pursuit of 216, alongside Boycott. The Queen was able to enjoy Boycott at his most obdurate, as he painstakingly added 64 with Barber, who was bowled by Motz just before the close. Titmus came in as nightwatchman, and stumps were drawn with England 64 for 1.

Only three hours' play were possible on the final day, which made things interesting. New Zealand were unable to put much pressure on England – but the clock could. They still needed more than 100 after the tea interval, but at last Boycott broke the shackles. In a little over two hours, he put on 126 with Dexter, and though Boycott was dismissed with 20 still needed for victory, England won with 15 minutes remaining, thus claiming the series.

The third and final Test, at Leeds, was extremely one-sided. Edrich replaced Boycott, and Barrington was released from purgatory. When England decided to bat, both made up for lost time. Edrich made 310 not out, the first triple-century for England since 1938, hitting 52 fours and five sixes. Barrington's contribution to their second-wicket stand of 369 was 163. England declared at 546 for 4, and their spinners took control. New Zealand were bowled out for 193 (Illingworth 4 for 42) and 166 (Titmus 5 for 19) as England swept the series.

South Africa, fortunately, made for much stiffer opposition. England clung on for a draw, seven wickets down, in the first Test at Lord's, then received an utter Pollocking in the second at Trent Bridge. Graeme scored 125 and 59; Peter took 10 wickets in the match. He then took seven in another draw at The Oval, where Colin Bland hit a second-innings century, as the tourists claimed a famous series victory.

The sublime Sobers

England v West Indies at Lord's, 1966

West Indies 269 (S. M. Nurse 64; K. Higgs 6–91) **and 369 for 5 declared** (G. S. Sobers 163*, D. A. J. Holford 105*). **England 355** (T. W. Graveney 96, J. M. Parks 91; W. W. Hall 4–106) **and 194 for 4** (C. Milburn 126*). **Drawn.**

Here they were again: Hunte, Kanhai, Butcher, Sobers with the bat. Hall, Griffith, Gibbs – and Sobers – with the ball. Worrell had retired, so Sobers took over the captaincy, and was immediately successful in the first Test. After his 161 set up a total of 484, supported by Hunte's 135, Manchester lived up to its reputation for spin as England were turned over twice. Gibbs took 5 for 37 as the hosts capitulated for 167 and followed on 317 behind. They fared a little better second time around, Colin Milburn's 94 on debut lifting them to 277, but Gibbs's 5 for 69 made sure West Indies did not have to bat again.

England fared much better in the second Test but, in truth, they were a team in transition, at least with the ball; Trueman, the last of their great 1950s seamers, had hung up his boots, and their attack at Lord's was Jeff Jones, a left-arm pacer from Glamorgan; Ken Higgs, Lancashire's under-rated seamer; Barry Knight, the Essex all-rounder; and Titmus the off-spinner. Basil D'Oliveira played a supporting role. Compared with previous England bowling line-ups, it was not an attack to instil fear in the hearts of opponents. Bowling West Indies out for 269, then, was quite an achievement; Higgs's 6 for 91 was his best Test bowling performance. Seymour Nurse was the only West Indian to make a half-century. England's batting was encouraging, too. Though Milburn went early, lbw to Hall, Boycott and Graveney brought up 100; Graveney, recalled by England after three years' absence, made a chanceless 96 before edging an attempted square cut off Hall. Parks hit out, putting on 59 for the ninth wicket with Higgs, and extending England's lead to 86. Higgs dismissed Joey Carew for the second time in the match, and West Indies reached the rest day one down and 68 behind.

Fourth day – 20 June

England's bowling quintet at Lord's was neither famed nor fabled, so it was a surprise that they had half the West Indians out, just nine ahead, by the end of the fourth morning. But the Queen was treated to a commanding, attractive century from Garry Sobers in a big partnership with David Holford who, at the close of play, was well on the way to his only Test century. Colin Cowdrey became the Queen's most-encountered cricketer: they had now met eight times.

Things continued to go well for England's hotch-potch bowling attack when play resumed on Monday morning. Knight soon got Hunte, and Higgs trapped Butcher in front, to make it 25 for 3. Kanhai and Nurse rallied West Indies through a stand of 66, but when they fell within minutes of each other, the tourists had lost five wickets and were just nine ahead. England looked like wrapping things up that day, but there was one more obstacle to overcome: Sobers. The West Indian captain embarked upon an immense, unbroken sixth-wicket stand of 274 in more than five hours, marshalling the unheralded David Holford to his only Test century – indeed, he only made three in his whole first-class career. The runs came at such a pace that West Indies, 202 ahead at the end of the fourth day, were able to declare just before lunch on the fifth, setting England 284 to win in two sessions. This sporting decision was very typical of Sobers – it wouldn't always pay off, as he learned in Trinidad in 1968, but England met it in the spirit intended. Milburn, in only his second Test, launched into a wondrous display of big hitting, continuing to play his strokes even after Hall dismissed Cowdrey and Parks with successive balls. At 67 for 4, Graveney defended while Milburn went on the attack. A final score of 197 for 4 in 55 overs may seem sedate by today's standards, but in the sixties it was almost mind-boggling. It was the closest England got to victory before the final Test at The Oval, by which time the series was dead.

The slower, spin-friendly pitches that were supposed to nullify the threat of Hall and Griffith at Nottingham and Leeds only played into the hands of Gibbs and Sobers, the latter switching to left-arm spin to make best use of the conditions. Big West Indian totals gave Sobers licence to set attacking fields and let the spinners twirl away. In the third Test, West Indies conceded a lead of 90 – England had bolstered their bowling with Snow and Illingworth, and Graveney hit his third century in successive Tests at Trent Bridge – but then racked up 482, with Butcher making an unbeaten 200. There was plenty of time to bowl England out a second time. In the fourth Test at Headingley, Sobers made 174 and then took 5 for 41 in England's first innings; Gibbs claimed 6 for 39 in the follow-on, and the series went to the visitors. England were able to turn the tables in the fifth Test, twice dismissing the jaded West Indies either side of a remarkable innings of 527. They had been 166 for 7 before John Murray's 112 from No. 9, and his last-wicket stand of 128 with Snow, who made 59.

Out-spinning the Indians

England v India at Lord's, 1967

India 152 (A. L. Wadekar 57) **and 110** (R. Illingworth 6–29). **England 386** (T. W. Graveney 151, K. F. Barrington 97; B. S. Chandrasekhar 5–127). **England won by an innings and 124 runs.**

After the successful two-tourist summer of 1965, another double-header was scheduled for 1967: India visited from April to July, and Pakistan from June to September. India brought the four spinners who would dominate their bowling attack for the next decade: Bishan Bedi, a Punjabi slow-left armer who had made his debut at home against West Indies the previous winter; Bhagwat Chandrasekhar, a leg-spinner from Karnataka who had bowled well when England visited India in early 1964; another Karnatakan, off-spinner Erapalli Prasanna, making his Test comeback after two games in 1962; and Srinivas Venkataraghavan, from Madras, who also bowled off-breaks. He was the first of the quartet to grab hold of a Test, taking 12 for 152 against New Zealand at Delhi in March 1965. Chandrasekhar took 11 for 235 in a losing cause against West Indies at Bombay 18 months later – but Bedi and Prasanna were yet to make their mark.

There were high hopes for all four in England, if only the pitches – and the Indian batters – would back them up. Unfortunately, a wet spring and green surfaces conspired against India. Their batters had few answers to seam attacks on lively tracks – Kent and Surrey beat them, and they came up against a rampant Snow who took 5 for 38 for MCC at Lord's – and India's captain, the Nawab of Pataudi, didn't dare pick all four spinners at once. He tried three in a rainy draw at Worcester, and again at Cardiff, where Prasanna took 5 for 21, then at The Oval, where they were outbowled by Pat Pocock, and at Southport, where they bowled almost all India's overs. But they could get nothing out of the first Test pitch at Leeds; Venkataraghavan was omitted, and the others had combined figures of 2 for 340 as England racked up 550 for 4. Boycott scored an unbeaten 246 in over nine hours, for which he would lose his place in the second Test (as Barrington had in 1965). D'Oliveira's 109 was more sprightly. India capitulated for 164, then made 510 in the follow-on, with Pataudi making 148, but England still won by six wickets.

Dennis Amiss replaced Boycott at Lord's, where the pitch seemed certain to spin later in the match. India put faith in the same three spinners and chose to bat, but were blown away for 152 on a dismal and damp first day; Dilip Sardesai had his hand broken during a whirlwind spell from Snow. England ended the first day two down but only 45 behind; their main obstacle over the next two days was bad weather, which routinely interrupted their progress. Barrington made 97 before missing Chandrasekhar's googly, but England reached 307 for 3 – more than double India's score – thanks to Graveney's sublime 151. They lost 5 for 27 after lunch on day three, Chandrasekhar taking 5 for 127.

Fourth day – 26 June

India, beginning their second innings, needed 234 to draw level with England and force a fourth innings. But after John Snow made the early breakthrough, Ray Illingworth and new captain Brian Close – both bowling off-breaks – ran through the visitors so quickly that the Queen arrived just as the match was drawing to a conclusion. She was introduced to the teams by Sir Alec Douglas-Home, prime minister from 1963 to 1964, and by then president of MCC.

Not for the first time, the Queen was a little late to witness the best of the cricket. India's openers strode out on Monday morning, facing a mammoth task: 234 were needed just to make England bat again, and the tourists were without the services of Sardesai. Budhi Kunderan found himself promoted from No. 8 to makeshift opener and clung on bravely as wickets fell around him. Farokh Engineer was the first to go, caught off Amiss for 8; then Ajit Wadekar joined Kunderan in a stand of 52. But the pitch was offering plenty of turn, and when Wadekar was bowled by Illingworth for 19, the procession began. Close's off-breaks dismissed Borde and Pataudi through close catches, then Illingworth removed Rusi Surti, Venkataraman Subramanya and Prasanna in a trice. Kunderan was eighth out, for a dogged 47 which earned him the opener's berth for the final Test. Illingworth's final figures were 22.3–12–29–6, the best return of his England career.

India took their frustration out on Derbyshire (Chandrasekhar taking 7 for 59 in the first innings, Prasanna 6 for 64 in the second), but an innings defeat to Yorkshire was followed by a remarkable game at Leicester, where John Cotton's career-best 9 for 29 bowled India out for 63. It was only at The Oval, in the third Test, that Pataudi bit the bullet and selected all four spinners. They took 18 England wickets, but the home spinners (Close, Illingworth and Robin Hobbs) took 15, and India lost by 132 runs. Bedi, Chandrasekhar, Prasanna and Venkataraghavan would go on to take 43 five-wicket innings in 231 Tests between them.

Hanif holds out

England v Pakistan at Lord's, 1967

England 369 (K. F. Barrington 148, T. W. Graveney 81, B. L. D'Oliveira 59) **and 241 for 9 declared** (B. L. D'Oliveira 81). **Pakistan 354** (Hanif Mohammad 187*, Asif Iqbal 76) **and 88 for 3. Drawn.**

After England's whitewash of India in the first half of the season, Pakistan were expected to present sterner opposition. For the most part, they did, though the series score (2–0 to England) might not suggest so. Where India had strength in spin, Pakistan had a capable all-round squad, with more accomplished batting. The leaders were the Gujarat-born brothers, Hanif and Mushtaq Mohammad; both were well known to English audiences, having toured England before. So had Saeed Ahmed, who hit a carefree century at Eastbourne in the opening fixture of the tour. Majid Khan, an alumnus of Cambridge University and the cousin of future Pakistan star Imran Khan, hit a hundred at Canterbury, where Derek Underwood took 10 wickets in the match, and another against Middlesex at Lord's. He and Hanif were in supreme form by the time the first Test came along.

Close won the toss at Lord's and decided England would bat first, but they quickly lost Milburn, caught behind off the young seamer Asif Iqbal. Asif was, in his first few years of international cricket, something of a jack of all trades. He batted at No. 10 and No. 3 against Australia in his first Test, at Karachi in 1964, scoring 41 and 36; in a return fixture at Melbourne he went in at No. 7, then eight – where he remained for a time, until he ticked off No. 5 and No. 6 back home in Pakistan. He opened the bowling in all his early Tests, taking 18 wickets in a three-match series in New Zealand. Milburn's dismissal brought in Barrington, who dominated so completely that Pakistan only took one more wicket that day. Barrington eventually made 148 out of 369, supported by 81 from Graveney and D'Oliveira's 59. Pakistan, struggling in drizzle that frequently brought play to a halt, came undone against Higgs and Snow, and slowed almost to a standstill. They were in great trouble at 139 for 7, but Hanif began a brave rearguard, diligently supported by Asif, now batting at No. 9. By the rest day, Hanif had reached 102 in nearly six hours, and Asif had managed 56.

Fourth day – 31 July

It was the first time the Queen saw two Tests in the same summer. After missing almost all the action a month earlier, she now saw one of the great rearguards, as Hanif Mohammad scored 187 not out to bring Pakistan almost to parity. His partner for much of the innings was the as-yet-unheralded Asif Iqbal, who scored 76 at No. 9. England teetered to 95 for 4 after shaking hands with the Queen; Ken Barrington met her for the ninth time, passing Colin Cowdrey's record.

Pakistan began the Monday with hopes of continuing their recovery. Hanif and Asif had rescued them, but they were still 133 behind, and after an hour they lost Asif, caught off Illingworth for 76, his highest Test score to date. The wicketkeeper Wasim Bari, on debut, helped Hanif add a further 41, and then came an extraordinary last-wicket stand worth 44, of which No. 11 Salim Altaf made just two. Hanif remained unbeaten on 187, scored in nine hours – his team's highest individual innings against England. England's lead had been trimmed to 15 and Pakistan were buoyant. After meeting the Queen during the innings break, they took four wickets before the hosts could raise 100, and the match was finely balanced at the close of play, England being 146 ahead with six wickets in hand.

England rallied through D'Oliveira, whose 81 not out enabled Close to declare soon after lunch on the final day, setting Pakistan 257 from 62 overs, a target they decided against chasing. In fact, they defended as though their very lives depended on the draw, scoring just 88 for the loss of three wickets; more than half the overs they faced were maidens.

But it was not through lack of enterprise that Pakistan lost the second Test at Trent Bridge. Having chosen to bat, they managed a feeble 140, and not even a thunderstorm so immense that the fire brigade had to pump the field clear of water could arrest England's march to victory. Barrington scored another century, and Close – with England running out of time to force the win – felt obliged to declare with a lead of 112. His gamble paid off, as Underwood tore through the Pakistanis just as he had done for Kent; only Saeed had any answer, striking a fluent 68.

Pakistan were outgunned at The Oval too, despite managing 216 in their first innings. Barrington's third hundred of the series set England on their way to 440, and Higgs's 5 for 58 reduced Pakistan to 65 for 8 in their second innings, still 159 short of making England bat again. Miraculously, Asif smashed 146 in a ninth-wicket partnership of 190 with Intikhab Alam that would remain a world record for 30 years. England had to make 32 to win, which they duly did – but Asif would never bat outside Pakistan's top seven again, in a Test career lasting 13 more years.

The Australians are skittled

England v Australia at Lord's, 1968

England 351 for 7 declared (C. Milburn 83, K. F. Barrington 75).
Australia 78 (D. J. Brown 5–42) **and 127 for 4** (I. R. Redpath 53).
Drawn.

Colin Cowdrey had already surpassed Godfrey Evans's world record
of 91 Test appearances and the 1968 Ashes series began amidst
excited anticipation for his 100th match. After he had succeeded
May as captain in 1960, he had seen it pass through the hands
of Dexter, Smith and Close, and it now fell to him once again.
On Thursday 30 May, an honour was bestowed on Cowdrey that
no England captain had received since Peter May: an invitation to
Buckingham Palace. May had gone to Sunday lunch; Cowdrey was
entertained at a cocktail party. No doubt he met the Queen, for
the ninth time, but he had to share her company with (among
others) George Burton, chief executive of Fisons Fertilisers, Cranley
Onslow, MP for Woking, the violinist Alan Loveday and Leonard
Russell, literary editor of the *Sunday Times*. Cowdrey was amiable
and a conversationalist, but he probably took refuge in conversation
with Bill Lawry, the Australian captain, who was invited too.

The Australians, who still held the Ashes, had a quiet start to
their tour – it rained for most of May, though John Gleeson and
Ashley Mallett had time to spin them to victory at Northampton
– and they seemed somewhat undercooked when they arrived
at Manchester for the first Test. The now-customary Old Trafford
turner awaited them, but they won the toss and made 357. Lawry
scored 81 and Doug Walters and Ian Chappell hit half-centuries.
England disintegrated after Edrich and Boycott's opening stand of
86; they could not even double that score as occasional off-spinner
Bob Cowper registered 4 for 48, his best Test figures. Walters's
second-innings 86 held Australia together as Pocock claimed 6 for
76, and England were set 413. They never looked in with a chance,
subsiding to a 159-run defeat, despite D'Oliveira's unbeaten 87.

It was a surprise, then, when England were so dominant at Lord's. Had it not rained, they might well have levelled the series – but the weather accounted for more than half the scheduled play. England brought back Milburn and Barrington, and both made attractive half-centuries. Milburn's 83 was savage – Cowdrey had promoted him to No. 3 – and though Gleeson denied him a century, the knock was his most memorable Test innings. England put up 351 for 7 before declaring – a decision more or less forced by the rain, which pushed the innings to the close of the third day.

Fourth day – 24 June

The Monday of the Lord's Test in 1968 was one of the most exciting days of cricket attended by the Queen. Beset by rain, and with only two days remaining, Colin Cowdrey declared England's first innings on 351 for 7. Australia were skittled for 78, the hero being Warwickshire's David Brown, who took 5 for 42. In the follow-on, captain Bill Lawry and Ian Redpath dug deep to put on 50 by the close. Cowdrey and Ken Barrington met the Queen for the 10th time.

After the rest day, Cowdrey declared on the overnight total, and Australia were confronted by a pitch made lively by Sunday rain. They responded with their lowest total in almost two decades. The ball seamed and swung, the fielders drew close, and every catch went to hand. David Brown removed the openers, Lawry and Ian Redpath. Snow got rid of Cowper. Then, from 46 for 3, Brown and Knight ran through the rest, rolling Australia for 78. They followed on 273 behind, but Lawry and Redpath fought hard, raising 50 by stumps.

Rain prevented play until after three o'clock on the fifth day. England had only removed Lawry by tea, and played out time against Underwood, whose remarkable figures were 18–15–8–2.

Cowdrey's 100th Test match came at Birmingham, where England were again in the ascendancy but thwarted by the elements. Australia had lost their first game of the tour, when Illingworth took eight wickets for Yorkshire, and the off-spinner joined forces with

Underwood at Edgbaston. It was Cowdrey who made the headlines, though, first by passing 7,000 Test runs (a record only previously attained by Wally Hammond), then by reaching his 21st Test century on the second morning. He set Australia 330 to win in a day plus 10 minutes – but rain came at lunch on the final day, and that was that.

Illingworth and Underwood shared 13 wickets in the drawn fourth Test at Headingley, and England memorably drew the series at The Oval. D'Oliveira scored his famous 158, eventually earning him a recall for the ill-fated tour of South Africa that winter, and Underwood cleaned up the Australians – after the spectators had cleaned up the wet ground – with 7 for 50 in the final innings.

Illingworth leads
with bat and ball

England v West Indies at Lord's, 1969

West Indies 380 (C. A. Davis 103, G. S. Camacho 67, R. C. Fredericks 63; J. A. Snow 5–114) **and 295 for 9 declared** (C. H. Lloyd 70, R. C. Fredericks 60, G. S. Sobers 50). **England 344** (R. Illingworth 113, J. H. Hampshire 107, A. P. E. Knott 53) **and 295 for 7** (G. Boycott 106, P. J. Sharpe 86). **Drawn.**

The third split international season of the sixties came in 1969, when a visit from West Indies was followed by one from New Zealand – arguably the wrong way round to give the tourists conditions best matching their strengths, but a heatwave, which began in June, rendered such niceties academic. West Indies were captained by Sobers, which usually meant attractive, sporting contests and an aversion to boring draws. The early season rain ruined most of May's matches, though John Shepherd had taken 8 for 40 against Gloucestershire on a wet pitch at Bristol, the best return of his long career, and Northamptonshire managed a win over the tourists.

The batters made a good start to June, when Joey Carew, Clive Lloyd, Charlie Davis and Basil Butcher made centuries, but that form deserted them in the first Test at Manchester. Boycott made 128 in an England total of 413 occupying nearly 200 overs; several catches were dropped and, in the circumstances, Shepherd's 5 for 104 was a heroic effort. From the moment Snow dismissed Roy Fredericks with the first ball of the innings, West Indies were in a mess. They were dismissed for 147, then followed on and made 275. England needed less than five overs to complete a 10-wicket win – a great success for Ray Illingworth in his first match as captain.

West Indies batted first at Lord's, taking most of the first two days to score 380. Openers Fredericks and Steve Camacho began with 106, before Davis made the first century of an all too brief Test career which would see him score 1,301 runs at an average of 54, including four hundreds. Snow took 5 for 114, and there was still life in the pitch when England were reduced to 46 for 4 by the close of the second day; Sobers had bowled very fast in a spell of 11–8–9–2. Sharpe soon fell next morning, bringing wicketkeeper Alan Knott to the wicket alongside debutant John Hampshire, whose selection had raised eyebrows – he had hit just 10 centuries in eight years of county cricket, and had not yet reached three figures in the 1969 season. His plucky 107 was supported by 53 from Knott, then Illingworth, who had never previously made more than 50. He was 97 not out at the end of the third day and had to sweat on his century through the rest day.

Fourth day – 30 June

Ray Illingworth, named England captain at the start of the series, made his first Test hundred and reduced the West Indies' lead to 36. Roy Fredericks made a second handsome half-century in the match, before Clive Lloyd and Garry Sobers picked up the scoring rate in an attempt to set up a declaration.

Illingworth brought up his landmark first thing on Monday, and the West Indies' lead was kept to 36. Fredericks and Camacho extended it to 109 before they were separated, but D'Oliveira got Camacho and Davis in the same over, forcing Fredericks and Butcher to rebuild. They added 55 before both fell to Illingworth. Conscious that his team needed to win to have a chance of taking the series, Sobers told Lloyd they must attack. Lloyd's 70 took only 88 balls, and West Indies reached the close at 247 for 6, a lead of 283.

Sobers didn't dare declare overnight. No doubt he was still smarting from the criticism he'd received for setting England 215 in 165 minutes in Trinidad the previous year. He batted on for an hour, before declaring on reaching his half-century. England needed 332 in five hours. It says a lot for England's positive approach that they reached 295 for 3, despite Boycott taking two and a half hours over his first 50 runs, though he accelerated as he drew closer to his hundred. Gibbs bowled unchanged for 41 overs, taking only 1 for

93. Sharpe had the right idea, hitting a quick 83, but England paid for Boycott's early caution, and could not manage 61 from the last 10 overs.

West Indies could only draw the series at Leeds, but first came their now-infamous trip to Northern Ireland. They had agreed to play a brace of one-day matches in Strabane and Belfast, but the first did not go according to plan. They were bowled out for 25 and lost by nine wickets. What England's bowlers had twice spent more than a hundred overs trying to do at Lord's, Alec O'Riordan and Doug Goodwin managed in just 25.3 overs.

The third Test at Headingley was an absorbing game. England made 223 and bowled West Indies out for 161. In the second innings, after Boycott registered a duck, every England batter made between 16 and 39 in a total of 240, which set the visitors a target of 303. The chase was thrilling. Camacho and Davis made half-centuries and West Indies reached 219 for 3, but for once Sobers could produce no magic, and they collapsed, losing by 30 runs.

Double spin scuppers the Kiwis

England v New Zealand at Lord's, 1969

England 190 (R. Illingworth 53) **and 340** (J. H. Edrich 115). **New Zealand 169** (R. Illingworth 4–37, D. L. Underwood 4–38) **and 131** (D. L. Underwood 7–32). **England won by 230 runs.**

New Zealand began their tour with three festival-style games, against D. H. Robins's XI at Eastbourne, London New Zealand CC at The Oval, and the International Cavaliers at Luton. The third match was something of a curio: the International Cavaliers were a by-invitation team made up of famous cricketers from around the world; they had beaten the touring West Indians in 1966, and did the same to the 1969 New Zealanders. Ted Dexter, his England career over by this time, scored 73 and Trueman – likewise retired – took three wickets as the tourists went down by 38 runs. But New Zealand came back hard, defeating Scotland by an innings before drawing five county games. They only came unstuck on a turning track against Essex in mid-July, which boded ill for the Test series.

The pitch for the first Test at Lord's was guaranteed to support the spinners as the match wore on, so England picked Underwood to partner Illingworth and rested Snow. Crucially, they won the toss and batted. Scoring freely was immensely difficult, especially early on against Dayle Hadlee, whose father Walter had captained New Zealand's 1949 team. Only Illingworth made much headway with a gutsy half-century, and the ball was already turning by the time England's innings ended on 190.

Second day – 25 July

The Queen broke with tradition as monarch for only the second time, by attending the Lord's Test on the second day,

a Friday, when New Zealand replied to England's first innings of 190 by scoring only 169. Spin quickly became the focus of the day, as Derek Underwood and Ray Illingworth shared eight wickets to secure England a lead.

New Zealand lost Glenn Turner early on day two, caught behind by Knott off debutant Alan Ward, but it was not until Ward got rid of Congdon, shortly after lunch, that England seized the initiative. From 101 for 3, Illingworth and Underwood cut a swathe through the rest; no one after Congdon made more than 23. England had failed with the bat, but New Zealand struggled to capitalise, conceding a lead of 21, which the hosts doubled by the close.

The third day was all about the batters: Boycott, desperate to atone for a first-innings duck, made just 15 in the two hours before lunch, but Edrich compiled a watchful century as England reached 234 for 2. Illingworth instructed the middle order to accelerate after tea, but it was easier said than done against the slow left-armer Hedley Howarth, and England reached stumps at 301 for 9. On the fourth day, Knight and Ward put together a defiant last-wicket partnership of 40, which set the visitors 362 in the best part of two days – a hopeless mission on a spin-friendly pitch. Ward took the first wicket quickly and from then on Underwood was irresistible. He took the next seven wickets, and only a late flourish from Motz got New Zealand past 100. Turner carried his bat in a four-hour 43 out of 131, and England won by an innings.

The second Test at Nottingham was ruined by rain, which accounted for nearly two whole days' play. A positive result was out of the question, but the batters prospered during what cricket there was. Congdon and Brian Hastings shared a third-wicket stand of 150 in New Zealand's first-innings 294, and Boycott made another duck in England's reply. Edrich and Sharpe, though, made the most of their opportunity. Both made centuries in a partnership of 249; Sharpe's 111 was his only hundred in 12 Test appearances which yielded 786 runs at an average of 46. England declared at 451 for 8, but only 23 overs were possible after that. The fickle weather continued throughout the third Test at The Oval, but the frequent showers only served Underwood, a lethal bowler on wet pitches:

he took 6 for 41 in New Zealand's first innings and 6 for 60 in their second. England's first-innings lead of 92 was priceless, and they were hardly challenged in their pursuit of 138.

By the end of 1969, the Queen had been to the cricket – or the cricket had come to her, in one form or another – every year since 1951. But a difficult question was now being asked: would she meet the South Africans at the Lord's Test of 1970? The South African rugby team visited the UK in the winter of 1969/70, playing more than two dozen games amid substantial anti-Apartheid protests. The 'Stop the 70 Tour' campaign was in full swing by the new year. For many people – and not just cricket fans – the South African government's objection to England bringing D'Oliveira, a non-white player, on their tour of 1968/69 drew a line in the sand for South Africa's continued participation in international sport. The 1970 tour was cancelled, and the Queen did not attend the England v Rest of the World series that replaced it.

A miserable Monday

England v Pakistan at Lord's, 1971

England **241 for 2 declared** (G. Boycott 121*) **and 117 for 0** (R. A. Hutton 58*, B. W. Luckhurst 53). **Pakistan 148. Drawn.**

The Queen, and indeed the entire Royal Family, steered clear of cricket altogether in 1970, the first fallow year of her reign. But she made sure to watch both Pakistan and India when they visited in 1971. Pakistan had a squad with a familiar look to it. Five of their Test team had played for counties: Asif Iqbal (Kent), Intikhab Alam (Surrey), Majid Khan (Glamorgan), Mushtaq Mohammad (Northamptonshire) and Sadiq Mohammad (Essex). Zaheer Abbas would play for Gloucestershire in 1972.

In the build-up to the Tests, Northamptonshire beat Pakistan by seven wickets, assisted by Mushtaq, representing his county over country, who scored 96 runs and took three wickets. Cambridge University also got the better of them, thanks to 11 wickets from the seamer John Spencer, who spent a dozen seasons at Sussex. Gloucestershire, were trounced just before the first Test. Birmingham served up a shirt-front of a pitch, on which Pakistan accumulated 608 in just over two days. Asif Iqbal and Mushtaq both scored centuries, but the big news was Zaheer's 274, Pakistan's first double-century against England, who were then in trouble at 148 for 6. Knott's 116 rescued the situation somewhat, but he could not avert the follow-on. Brian Luckhurst's unbeaten 108 had got England close to parity by the time rain killed off the last five hours of play. Pakistan might reasonably have felt they were robbed of victory.

If the weather had spoiled the climax at Edgbaston, it ruined the whole game at Lord's. Less than half the scheduled overs could be bowled, and a result never looked remotely achievable. No play was possible until after tea on the first day, but England reached 118 for 0 by the close. There were a few overs the next day, during which England added 15, but then it rained all afternoon, and all of Saturday too.

71

Fourth day – 21 June

Just a couple of hours' play were possible on the Monday of a depressingly damp match. Geoffrey Boycott completed his century, and John Edrich scored 37 before being caught off Pervez Sajjad – the only wicket of the day. Ray Illingworth made a token declaration at 241 for 2, and Pakistan were 49 for 0 at the close.

Even the rest day was wet, and the miserable weather continued into Monday, when play eventually got underway at half past two, just in time for the Queen's arrival. Boycott reached his hundred, and England soon declared at 241 for 2. Pakistan's openers, Aftab Gul and Sadiq, reached 49 for 0 by stumps.

The fifth day confounded expectations by offering some entertaining cricket, despite there being no prospect of a win for either team. Pakistan reached 117 for 3, then collapsed. John Price, playing on his home ground, dismissed Wasim Bari and Asif Masood with successive balls, but was denied the opportunity of a hat-trick when Pervez, the number eleven, did not come out to bat because he was ill. Richard Hutton, given his Test debut on the back of a ferocious 189 against the tourists a few days earlier, removed Mushtaq for his first international wicket, and was asked to open the batting with Luckhurst – and both scored unbeaten half-centuries.

And so, via Wales (where Pakistan lost) and Scotland (where they won) to Leeds, with all to play for. The third Test was a classic. Boycott led the way for England, after they had slipped to 10 for 2, with his third Test century in a row; he received sterling support from D'Oliveira, who made 74. In response to England's 316, Pakistan played confidently, with 72 from Zaheer and 57 from Mushtaq – and 63 from wicketkeeper Wasim Bari, down the order (he had never previously made more than 19 in Tests). He had a match to remember, finishing with eight dismissals all told, which equalled the Test record. Pakistan's 350 gave them a lead of 34, and they were in control after Luckhurst completed a pair. England did not take the lead until the morning of day four, and were in trouble at 142 for 5. Then Illingworth, on 1, was dropped by Asif Iqbal at gully. It proved a turning point. The England captain made 45, adding 106 with D'Oliveira, who played attractively for 72. Salim took the new ball and skittled four of the last five for the addition of 16 runs, giving Pakistan a target of 231. The pitch was now conducive to spin, and the visitors' chances seemed negligible when they fell to 65 for 4. Sadiq, though, took control with a commanding 91, putting on 95 with Asif Iqbal; Pakistan needed 71 with six wickets in hand. Gifford coaxed a stumping off Asif, D'Oliveira picked off Intikhab – and then had Sadiq, caught and bowled. It was the key wicket; Peter Lever wiped out the tail in no time to seal a 25-run victory.

Out-spun by the Indians

England v India at Lord's, 1971

England 304 (J. A. Snow 73, A. P. E. Knott 67; B. S. Bedi 4–70) **and 191** (J. H. Edrich 62; S. Venkataraghavan 4–52); **India 313** (A. L. Wadekar 82, G. R. Viswanath 68, E. D. Solkar 67; N. Gifford 4–84) **and 145 for 8** (S. M. Gavaskar 53; N. Gifford 4–43). **Drawn.**

As the Pakistanis departed England disappointed, the Indians arrived in confident mood. In the four years since their previous visit, their spin wizards had worked wonders. Prasanna had excelled in Australia and New Zealand in 1967/68, Bedi and Venkataraghavan had given New Zealand and Australia headaches in India in 1969/70, and all three had done well in the West Indies in 1970/71. Chandrasekhar had been dropped, but his time was about to come. In fact, arriving during a hot, dry summer, the quartet enjoyed a feast of wickets, demolishing the counties innings by innings: Bedi took 6 for 29 against Middlesex, 5 for 64 at Birmingham, 6 for 93 at Cardiff and 7 for 111 against Surrey; Chandrasekhar claimed 5 for 65 against Middlesex, then 11 for 127 in the match at Leicester and 6 for 34 at Headingley; Venkataraghavan took 6 for 76 at Cardiff and 9 for 93 in the second innings against Hampshire at Bournemouth. Prasanna only took one five-for, against Sussex, and did not play a Test. But rarely can any set of visiting spinners have had such a harvest away from home – and in England, of all places. The first Test, at Lord's, was hotly anticipated.

First day – 22 July

The Queen saw the spectacle she had been denied during the Indians' previous visit: Bishan Bedi, Bhagwat Chandrasekhar and Srinivas Venkataraghavan sending down over after over of their twirly tricks. Boycott went early to the seamer Syed Abid Ali, but then it was spin from both ends for almost the whole day. Alan Knott's 67 saved England from total

collapse, but they were still up against it until John Snow hit a glorious fifty.

The Queen attended the first day of the series, and witnessed a compelling, see-sawing day of cricket. The advantage swung first one way then the other. The pitch was dry, and England won a crucial toss before bedding in for over 139 overs, of which India's seamers – Syed Abid Ali and Eknath Solkar – bowled just 23. They seemed innocuous enough, but they would infamously get under the skin of Boycott, who nicked behind off Abid Ali for three. Then Bedi and Chandrasekhar got to work, Bedi's slow left-armers ripping past the right handers' off-stump, and Chandrasekhar's leg-spin causing problems out of the rough. England had lost Luckhurst, Edrich, D'Oliveira and Amiss to the pair by the time 71 was on the board. Knott and Illingworth stopped the rot, using their feet to negate the spin. The lower order followed their example, but England were still precariously placed at 223 for 8 shortly after tea. But Snow, at number nine, with one Test fifty to his name, mixed stoic defence with enterprising strokeplay and made 73, to take England to 304 on the second morning.

India may have had superb spinners, but that had proven insufficient for a series win in 1967. This time, they came with batting power. Sardesai and Wadekar were capable enough, but the top order had received a significant boost through the addition of Gundappa Viswanath, who would go on to pass 6,000 Test runs, and Sunil Gavaskar, who reached 10,000. Wadekar, Viswanath and Solkar scored half-centuries to earn India a nine-run lead – and, crucially, neither Gifford nor Illingworth seemed capable of matching the Indian spinners. After Solkar dismissed Luckhurst for a single, the slow men cleaned England up for 191, leaving India a target of 183 to win their first Test in England. Thanks to Gavaskar's 53, they reached 101 for 3 before collapsing, and when Gavaskar was sixth out at 114, the match was in the balance. With India needing 38, and England requiring two wickets, the rain came.

The weather spoiled the second Test at Manchester, too. England again had the good fortune to win the toss and found themselves batting on a much more familiar pitch. In fact, it was Abid Ali's seamers which did the damage, reducing them to 41 for 4 before Luckhurst's 78 turned things round. Illingworth made 107 and Lever, playing in place of Snow, hit an unbeaten 88 at number nine to lift the total to 386. Lever tore through India, taking 5 for 70 to give England a lead of 174, before Luckhurst's century set the visitors a target of 420. They were 65 for 3 at the close of the fourth day – but the fifth was lost to the weather.

At The Oval, the Indians felt at home; the temperature was hot and the pitch bone dry. England still managed a respectable first innings of 355, with Knott making 90, and took a 71-run lead after Illingworth's 5 for 70. Then came the spell of the series. Chandrasekhar ruined the home batting with 6 for 38, bowling England out for 101 and leaving India a chaseable target of 173, which they achieved for the loss of six wickets. It was their first victory in England, at the 22nd attempt.

Missing Massie

London, 1972

The Ashes contest in England in 1972 has often been regarded as a watershed, marking the arrival of cricket's modern era: fast, hostile bowling on flat but true pitches, hard-hitting batters in the middle order, and the spinners getting a look-in only at the last.

Illingworth, who had masterminded England's aggressive reclaiming of the Ashes in Australia in 1970/71, was in charge again; his opposite number was Ian Chappell, who had first led his side in the controversial decider at Sydney. It was there that the enmity between the teams – or at least, between the England team and the Australian fans – erupted. Australia had not played an official Test since then and arrived in the UK with payback on their minds. But England got the better of them in the first Test at Manchester, despite Dennis Lillee's second-innings 6 for 66; Snow's eight wickets and Tony Greig's twin fifties on debut saw the hosts to a 1–0 lead.

Then, of course, came Lord's, and Bob Massie. In his first international appearance, the Australian took 8 for 84 and 8 for 53 with prodigious, unplayable swing; with Greg Chappell scoring a pugnacious 131 between Massie's virtuoso performances, England were condemned to an emphatic defeat early on the fourth afternoon – before the Queen could arrive. As usual, she had been at Ascot on the opening two days and was only scheduled to visit Lord's on the Monday after the rest day. England began that Monday on 86 for 9 and could set Australia only 81. The visitors had just enough time to spruce themselves up before being taken to Buckingham Palace for an evening reception – the fifth time a touring side had visited the Palace, but the first for an Australian party. After Underwood's 10 wickets claimed victory in the fourth Test at Headingley, and the Chappell brothers scored centuries in the fifth at The Oval, the series was drawn and the Ashes retained by England. By the end of the rubber, Massie was already more than halfway through his brief Test career, which barely saw out the year. After two Tests against Pakistan, he was never selected again.

On the road again

London, 1973

The Queen's cricket-watching peaked in the early seventies. For reasons unknown, having forgone her customary visit to watch England at Lord's in 1970 she also skipped matches in 1973, 1974 and 1979. It wasn't always on account of a more attractive engagement at Ascot. During New Zealand's visit in June 1973 – after they had lost an epic battle at Nottingham, scoring 440 in pursuit of 479 – she was absent from the first two days of the second Test while at the races, but instead of visiting Lord's afterwards, she travelled to Canada. As a result she missed Congdon making 175 in over eight hours (to add to his 176 at Trent Bridge) to give New Zealand a first-innings lead of 298. She missed Keith Fletcher batting the entire fifth day for a match-saving 178, and she missed Howarth bowling 70 overs to try and stop him. Instead, as New Zealand passed 500, she was boarding an Air Canada DC8, attended by Leslie Green (general manager of Heathrow Airport), Lord Boyd-Carpenter (chairman of the Civil Aviation Authority) and H. H. Kantor (vice president of Air Canada). She made up for her absence by hosting a reception at the Palace for the New Zealanders on the eve of their return home. They had lost the Test series 2–0 and the one-day series 1–0.

The West Indians visited in the second half of the summer, but the Lord's Test was scheduled – unusually – to be the third, and thus the last of the season. Having won the first, at The Oval, and after drawing the second at Edgbaston, the tourists came to Lord's needing only a draw to seal the series. They made sure of it with an immense first innings of 652 for 8 declared, which occupied most of the first two days. Kanhai batted almost all the first day for 157, Bernard Julien hit a swashbuckling 121, and Sobers contributed a sublime unbeaten 150. England, outfought, lost by an innings. The Queen was at Balmoral Castle on her annual summer holiday, though as England were collapsing on the final day, she was in Basingstoke, opening the new headquarters of the Automobile Association.

Knights, castles and cups

Barbados and Windsor, 1975

The Queen was not present at any cricket in 1974. When India played at Lord's in June, the Queen was at Ascot; when Pakistan came in August, she was at Balmoral. In both cases, she missed out on vintage performances: she would likely have seen Chris Old bowling India out for 42, and much of Underwood's 13 for 71 against Pakistan. She made up for the missed opportunities, though, with four cricket-related engagements the following year.

The Queen departed for the Americas on 16 February 1975. Her first stop was Bermuda, where her visit was threatened by a public employees' strike, which promised a boycott of the Royal party. Buses, ferries and rubbish collection were all brought to a halt by Bermuda's powerful trade union. She spent less than 48 hours there, before continuing to Barbados, where, on 19 February she bestowed a knighthood on Sobers in front of a crowd of 50,000 at the Garrison Savannah. He had retired from cricket the previous year, and had the rare distinction of being knighted without having to leave his hometown.

Back in England that spring, Mike Denness – who had taken over the reins on Illingworth's retirement – became the third England captain to receive a personal invitation from the Queen, and the first to visit Windsor Castle, where a lunch party was held. Among the other guests were the ballet dancer Beryl Grey, the playwright Alan Ayckbourn, the actor Arthur Lowe and the pentathlete Jim Fox. But a much larger reception was being planned. The first men's cricket World Cup was to be held in England in June, following the success of the inaugural women's edition two years previously. The eight participants were all members of the Commonwealth, so on the eve of the tournament, the Queen held a reception for the players at the Palace. While she did not attend the final to present the trophy – that responsibility fell to the Duke of Edinburgh – she met the great and the good of every major national team in world cricket.

The bank clerk goes to war

England v Australia at Lord's, 1975

England 315 (A. W. Greig 96, A. P. E. Knott 69, D. S. Steele 50; D. K. Lillee 4–84) **and 436 for 7** (J. H. Edrich 175, B. Wood 52). **Australia 268** (R. Edwards 99, D. K. Lillee 73*; J. A. Snow 4-66) **and 329 for 3** (I. M. Chappell 86, R. B. McCosker 79, G. S. Chappell 73*, R. Edwards 52*). **Drawn.**

The Australians who toured England in 1975 were a great team in the making. They had made it to the World Cup final where they lost to the impressive West Indies, who were a few steps ahead in their cricketing evolution. Having reclaimed the Ashes at home over the winter, Australia were confident when they set off around the counties in June. Kent surprised them in the opening game, chasing 354 on the last day, with Cowdrey making an unbeaten 151. But normal service was resumed thereafter – Ian Chappell was in the runs at Southampton, Lillee took 10 wickets and Walters made a barnstorming hundred against MCC (for whom Bob Woolmer bagged twin fifties and a hat-trick), then Greg Chappell scored 144 at Swansea. In the first Test at Birmingham, Australia made 359 before their pace bowlers skittled England twice, for 101 and 173. Lillee, Jeff Thomson and Max Walker all took five-wicket hauls. More runs were then piled on in the shires: Rick McCosker hit twin centuries at Hove and another at Leicester; the Chappells and Walters added to their tallies too.

At Lord's, England pulled two surprises. The first was Denness's resignation as captain and replacement by Greig. The second was their call-up of Northamptonshire's David Steele, hoping for a dose of nominative determinism. Grey-haired, bespectacled and 33 years old, Steele looked an unlikely saviour. His local butcher had promised him a lamb chop for every run he scored up to 50, and a steak per run after that. The tabloid press likened him to a bank clerk; Lillee nicknamed him "Groucho".

First day – 31 July

Four years and a week after her previous visit to a cricket match – the longest break of her reign so far – the Queen witnessed one of the great Ashes battles at Lord's. England were up against the supreme skill of Dennis Lillee, the fire of Jeff Thomson and the accuracy of Max Walker, and soon fell to 49 for 4. Then David Steele, plucked out of obscurity for his first Test at the age of 33, acted as England's rock, scoring 50, around which England built a decent total. Tony Greig made an attacking 96, and Alan Knott an impish 69, as the hosts fought back to post 315.

England were already in trouble at 10 for 1, having lost Barry Wood, when Steele made his way down the staircase to the Long Room – one flight too many, as it turned out, and he had to retrace his steps from the basement – and he soon found men falling all round him. Edrich and Amiss went the same way as Wood, leg before. Graham Gooch, fresh from a pair on Test debut at Edgbaston, departed for 6. Within an hour, it was 49 for 4, all four wickets falling to Lillee in his opening spell. When he tired, Steele and Greig painstakingly rebuilt the innings. It helped that Thomson was having a bad day (he bowled 17 no balls and four wides); they added 96 before Steele was bowled by Thomson for 50. Greig fell to Walker for 96, but Knott and Woolmer pressed on, and England ended the day on a respectable 313 for 9, to which they added two runs next morning.

Then came Snow. The Australians froze as he dismissed Alan Turner and the Chappells before 40 were on the board. Lever prised out McCosker and Walters, Greig removed Marsh, and Snow returned to bowl Walker. It was 81 for 7 when Ross Edwards began to wrest back control. His ebullient, counterattacking 99 included stands of 52 with Thomson, then 66 with Lillee. And when he departed – dismissed lbw playing across a yorker from Woolmer – Lillee took over, bashing his first Test half-century and extending it to 73 when Ashley Mallett was out, lbw to Steele's fourth ball in Test cricket. England, their lead cut to 47, made sure they couldn't lose by piling on 436, of which Edrich scored 175 and Steele a doughty

45. Australia were set 484 in more than eight hours on a pitch which had become utterly benign. McCosker, the Chappells and Edwards all passed 50 and the match was drawn.

The extraordinary events at Headingley more than outweighed the tedium of the final day at Lord's. Steele top-scored in both innings, with 73 and 92. After England had posted 288, the debutant left-arm spinner Phil Edmonds took 5 for 28 to skittle Australia for 135. England's 291 set a target of 445, which Australia were halfway towards attaining, for the loss of three wickets, when vandals – demanding the release of a convicted criminal, George Davis – ruined the pitch with knives and oil, forcing an abandonment. The Oval brought a third draw, Steele scoring 39 and 66, which secured the Ashes for Australia. Owing to the World Cup earlier in the summer, there wasn't time for a fifth Test.

Facing the four horsemen

England v West Indies at Lord's, 1976

England 250 (D. B. Close 60; A. M. E. Roberts 5–60) **and 254** (D. S. Steele 64; A. M. E. Roberts 5–63); **West Indies 182** (C. G. Greenidge 84, C. H. Lloyd 50; D. L. Underwood 5–39, J. A. Snow 4–68) **and 241 for 6** (R. C. Fredericks 138). **Drawn.**

It is strange to think that England's cricket team occasionally used to spend their winters at home. They were forced to do so in 1988/89, when several players' South African connections forced the cancellation of the visit to India, but before then, there was the odd winter in which no tour was arranged. This was the case three times in the fifties, three times in the sixties, and twice in the seventies. The last fallow off-season was 1975/76, though Derrick Robins arranged a private tour to South Africa, which cannot have enamoured the English to the rest of the cricketing world, and which most of England's Test regulars avoided.

West Indies, by now the pre-eminent side in international cricket, were not impressed. They were due to tour the UK in 1976, and two current England players had gone to South Africa: Frank Hayes, who had scored a century against them on Test debut at The Oval in 1973, and seamer Mike Hendrick, a regular pick (when fit). To make matters worse, Greig had said, in what what should have been a run-of-the-mill interview with the BBC on the eve of the series, "I'm not really sure they're as good as everyone thinks. If they get on top, they are magnificent cricketers. But if they're down, they grovel. And I intend, with the help of Closey and a few others, to make them grovel." Coming from a South Africa-born captain of England, this was all the motivation West Indies needed.

They had learned, during their chastening 1975/76 tour of Australia, what brutal pace could do. When they returned home, for a series against India, they focused on developing their fast-bowling attack. But it wasn't until their arrival in England that they first adopted their revolutionary tactic: four quick bowlers, and no specialist spinner. And then there was the unstoppable Viv Richards. His 232 in the series opener at Nottingham took him past 1,000 Test runs for the calendar year – in the first week of June. In reply to West Indies' 494, Steele made his first century for England, and Woolmer contributed 82, but four wickets for Wayne Daniel gave the visitors a lead of 162. Three hours later, they had extended it to 338, and gave themselves 78 overs to bowl England out; Edrich and Close shut up shop for a draw.

England decided to bat first at Lord's but it soon became clear that they were focused on surviving rather than scoring. They made 197 in 80.4 overs on the first day – the West Indian bowlers were unable to send down more than 14 overs an hour – with Andy Roberts taking 5 for 60. Next day, Underwood's unexpected 31 raised the total to 250, and when Old and Snow reduced the visitors to 40 for 3, England felt they were in charge. Greenidge and Lloyd held them up with a stand of 99, but then Underwood completed his impressive day by running through the rest, finishing with 5 for 39. By the close, England were 95 ahead, for the loss (to injury) of Wood. It rained all Saturday, severely denting the chances of a result.

Fourth day – 21 June

The Queen saw England's 'old timers', David Steele and Brian Close, try to keep the West Indian pace attack – Andy Roberts, Michael Holding, Bernard Julien and Vanburn Holder – at bay. But Roberts was irresistible, cutting through the middle order on his way to 10 wickets in the Test.

There was no sense of urgency about England's batting on the Monday. Pocock, the nightwatchman, was first to go, and Mike Brearley almost immediately followed. Steele and Close painstakingly took the score to 112, but Roberts, keeping up his speed and aggression, dismissed Steele, Woolmer and Knott to prevent England getting too far ahead. England were seven down at stumps and, after Roberts had taken his second five-for in the match, the West Indies required 323 in less than a day. They gave it a go, but ran out of time: another draw.

The West Indian victory at Manchester was one of their most memorable overseas successes. First came Greenidge's 134 out of 211 – the next-highest score was Collis King's 32 – and then followed Michael Holding's terrifying bouncer assault on Edrich and Close on the third evening. England's spirit was broken by the intimidation; they had received their Bodyline. They were all out for 71. Greenidge scored a second century, and Richards added one of his own, before Roberts destroyed England with 6 for 37. Another win followed at Leeds. And then, at The Oval, came the *piece de resistance*: 291 from Richards, and 14 wickets in the match for Holding. West Indies had played a four-prong seam attack in all but the third Test, rotating Roberts, Holding, Julien, Holder and Daniel until England were worn out with pace and worry.

A centenary in Australia

Australia v England at Melbourne, 1977

Australia 138 and 419 (R. W. Marsh 110*, I. C. Davis 68, K. D. Walters 66, D. W. Hookes 56; C. M. Old 4–104). **England 95** (D. K. Lillee 6–26, M. H. N. Walker 4–54) **and 417** (D. W. Randall 174, D. L. Amiss 64; D. K. Lillee 5–139). **Australia won by 45 runs.**

A couple of years before the Australian autumn of 1977, Hans Ebeling, a committee member of the Melbourne Cricket Club who had played one Test in 1934 and was now an occasional commentator, realised that it would soon be the 100th anniversary of the first Test match. That match, known today as Australia v England, was at the time billed as A Grand Combined Melbourne and Sydney XI v James Lillywhite's XI, to be played on the Richmond Police Paddock. Neither side was at full strength – there was no Fred Spofforth in the home team, and no W. G. Grace among the tourists, for a start – but it was a close and keenly-fought affair. The home side won by 45 runs, and over the next 100 years another 224 Tests were played between the teams, latterly for the Ashes. After Australia's triumph in England in 1975, the overall score was 88 wins to Australia, 71 to England, with 66 draws.

Ebeling was determined that Melbourne should hold a centenary fixture on the anniversary of the 1877 game at the same venue (the police paddock had become the Melbourne Cricket Ground). With the help of some rich benefactors, such as Qantas and Hilton, he planned an unforgettable, unmissable occasion: invitations were sent to the 244 living cricketers who had played in Tests between Australia and England; 218 attended. Here were Lindwall, Miller, Bradman and Benaud. May, Dexter, Compton and Edrich made the trip (Compton nearly didn't make it, having left his passport in Wales as he travelled to London; a breakneck return journey saw him arrive at Heathrow just in time). Colin McCool's house in Queensland had been cut off by floods; a helicopter landed on his front lawn to take him to the airport.

It was late in the Australian season and autumn showers had freshened the pitch on the eve of the Test. Greig had no hesitation in asking Australia to bat. His decision was soon vindicated. John Lever, who had made his debut in India a few months earlier, found swing to dismiss Ian Davis, and Bob Willis made the ball fly – including into the face of McCosker, fracturing his jaw and forcing him to stagger from the field. Old joined the party, running through the middle order, before Underwood finished off the innings with three cheap wickets, including Greg Chappell, who top-scored and was ninth out for 40, which took him almost four hours.

In reply to Australia's 138, England weathered the early storm from Lillee and Walker, losing only Woolmer: 29 for 1 at the close. But the second morning proved disastrous: Brearley was out after a single run had been added, and the floodgates burst open. Lillee and Walker shared all 10 wickets: only Brearley managed to bat longer than an hour, and no one made more than Knott's 18. The only cheerful moment was provided by Derek Randall, another debutant from the tour of India, who – during a brief stay for four runs – responded to a Lillee bouncer by doffing his cap and grinning back at his opponent. England were rolled for 95, with Lillee taking 6 for 26 in earning Australia a lead of 43, which they had extended to 147 for the loss of three wickets by stumps.

The third day belonged to the hosts. Walters made a dogged 66, and debutant David Hookes smashed 56 off 69 balls, including five fours in an over from Greig. England persevered, trying to prevent Rod Marsh reaching his first Test century, and when Lillee departed it was 353 for 8. With only Walker still to come, McCosker arrived at the crease, his head swathed in bandages. He clung on, even as Willis almost apologetically tested him with bouncers. Marsh had progressed to 95 by the time the rest day came. He reached his hundred on Monday morning and Australia declared on 419, setting England 463 to win in 11 hours. Woolmer soon went, but the limpet-like Brearley found a willing partner in Randall. The Nottinghamshire right-hander laid into Gary Gilmour, hitting him out of the attack, and wasn't afraid to go after Lillee either, cutting and hooking with force until he reached his first Test half-century. Lillee pinned Brearley lbw, and had Amiss dropped in the slips, but to his exasperation, Randall kept taking on his short ball. England were 191 for 2 going into the final day.

Fifth day – 17 March

The final day of the Centenary Test at Melbourne must have made up for all those dull, dreary Monday mornings the Queen had spent at Lord's. Dennis Lillee, at the peak of his powers, was on his way to 11 wickets in the match as England tried to reach 463 to win the historic game. He came up against the effervescent, eccentric Derek Randall, whose counterattacking 174 was one of the greatest fourth-innings performances in Tests.

It was one of the great days of Test cricket, beginning with England needing 272 more to win. Randall was by now in his element. After nudging Lillee off his hip for his first international century, he thrilled the crowd in his own bizarre, inimitable way. An eccentric at the best of times, he fell to the floor rubbing his head after being felled by one Lillee bouncer, then performed a backwards roll while playing another. And the more Lillee went for him, the more Randall chirped. "There's no point hitting me on my head, mate. There's nothing in it." As the afternoon drew on, Randall began singing to himself at the crease, much to the bemusement of Marsh. There was a stutter when Chappell bowled Amiss for 64, and Fletcher was caught behind for the second time in the match. Chappell then induced a nick from Randall, who was given out caught behind for 160. But Marsh, conceding that the ball had not carried, called the batter back. England were 330 for 4 as the Queen arrived, just as Randall was smashing four after four through the covers. But shortly before tea he was brilliantly caught by Gary Cosier, diving forward at short-leg off the leg-spinner Kerry O'Keeffe, for 174. As he made his way off the field, he headed to the wrong gate, and soon found himself on the threshold of the Royal box. "I did see the red carpet," Randall later admitted. "But I'd had a good day and I thought it were for me." At the interval, England needed 110 in two hours, with five wickets in hand.

When the Queen was introduced to the teams, everything went as expected – Walters, on meeting her for the fifth time, became the Australian who had met her most often – until she came to the end of the Australian line. Lillee, clutching an envelope and pen, asked for her autograph. She laughed, and gave him a "be off with you" gesture, before pausing to speak with McCosker, whose bandaged jaw made him look like a cartoon character with toothache.

Greig and Knott had brought the required runs down to 94 when Greig went the same way as Randall. Old edged Lillee to first slip, and Lever was trapped in front by O'Keeffe's googly, but Knott took England past 400. As the light began to fade, Underwood played on to Lillee, who then sealed victory – and his 11th wicket in the match – by pinning Knott in front of off stump. Australia had won by 45 runs, exactly the same margin as in the original Test a century earlier.

Brearley, Boycott and Botham

England v Australia at Nottingham, 1977

Australia 243 (R. B. McCosker 51; I. T. Botham 5–74) **and 309** (R. B. McCosker 107; R. G. D. Willis 5–88). **England 364** (A. P. E. Knott 135, G. Boycott 107; L. S. Pascoe 4–80) **and 189 for 3** (J. M. Brearley 81, G. Boycott 80*). **England won by seven wickets.**

Even as the Centenary Test was being played, the defections of Australian and English players to Kerry Packer's World Series Cricket were being arranged. For the summer's cricket, the only material change was the sacking of Greig – Packer's main man in the English camp – as England captain. His replacement, Brearley, was a fine county player, but had struggled to convert his domestic form into international runs. To many, he was simply inadequate as a Test batter, but to all, he was a superb captain.

England were further boosted by the news that three key Australia players were not coming. Lillee, who by then had 171 Test wickets at an average of 23, chose to rest his bad back, while Ian Chappell (5,234 runs at 47) and Edwards (1,171 runs at 40) were disinclined to tour; all three preferred to wait for the Packer games to begin later that year. England won the one-day series 2–1, with Australia shot out for 70 at Birmingham. The first Test at Lord's was drawn with the Australians teetering at 114 for 6 in pursuit of 226; had a day's worth of play not been lost to rain, England would most likely have won. Woolmer was their star performer, top scoring in both innings with 79 and 120. While Thomson looked fit and bowled well for eight wickets, he was outdone by Willis, who took 7 for 78 in Australia's first innings.

The Queen, inordinately busy – even by her standards – in her 25th year on the throne, missed the match altogether, even though it had been billed as the Silver Jubilee Test. She was at Ascot for the start of the Test, before travelling to north-west England on the Royal Train. At least she met a cricketer while there: the Right Reverend David Sheppard, by then Bishop of Liverpool. England followed her to Manchester for the second Test, where Woolmer continued his fine form, making 137 as the hosts took a lead of 140 then unleashed Underwood on a helpful pitch. His 6 for 66 gave the hosts a target of 79, which they knocked off easily. The Queen finally met up with the Ashes roadshow at Nottingham, where she was due to attend her first English Test match away from Lord's. Her first-day arrival was keenly anticipated by the Trent Bridge faithful – but perhaps not as much as Randall's.

First day – 28 July

In her only visit to an English Test away from Lord's, the Queen saw the international debut of a 21-year-old Somerset all-rounder named Ian Botham. He took 5 for 73, starting a record-breaking England career. The Queen would award him an OBE in 1992, knight him in 2007, and make him a life peer in 2020.

Randall was by now a local hero. He had scored 53 at Lord's, 79 at Manchester, and was set to play for England at his home ground. There was much excitement in Nottingham. What's more, the match signalled the return of Boycott, who had spent three years away from international cricket, but was ready for a comeback, having scored 103 for Yorkshire against the touring team.

Australia made a solid start after electing to bat, reaching 131 for 2 on the back of a tidy McCosker half-century. England had given a debut to the Somerset all-rounder Ian Botham, who claimed his first Test wicket when Greg Chappell edged a short, wide ball onto his wicket. Botham never looked back, adding Walters, Marsh, Walker and Thomson to bag 5 for 74. Australia were 155 for 8 before some late hits from O'Keeffe, whose 48 not out was the top score out of 243. After the Queen met the teams – including Walters, for the sixth time – England reached 9 for 0 by the close.

England were soon in bother against Thomson and Len Pascoe. Woolmer's third-ball duck brought Randall to the middle. Boycott quickly sent him back to the pavilion, calling him through for a suicidal single after hitting the ball back to the bowler. It was 82 for

5 before Boycott, finding an ally in Knott, turned the game around with a determined century; they stayed together until England had a substantial lead. Knott added his own hundred to put Australia 121 behind on first innings. Botham went wicketless second time around, but Willis's 5 for 88 left England needing 189 to win, despite McCosker's six-hour 107. Boycott and Brearley opened with 154 before Walker took three quick wickets; this brought Randall to the crease, and Boycott made sure to give him the winning hit.

Having made amends at Nottingham, Boycott became the hero at Leeds, where he was on the field for the entire match, as England won by an innings. His 191 was his 100th first-class hundred; Botham then took 5 for 21 to force the follow-on. Together they made sure England reclaimed the Ashes, which they did when Marsh hit a catch to Randall, who cartwheeled in celebration. The final Test at The Oval was ruined by rain, which ruled out nearly two days' worth of cricket. Australia had fashioned a lead of 171 thanks to their lower order but had little chance to build on it as the clock ran down.

First day but no play

England v Pakistan at Lord's, 1978

England 364 (I. T. Botham 108, G. R. J. Roope 69, G. A. Gooch 54, D. I. Gower 51). **Pakistan 105** (R. G. D. Willis 5–47, P. H. Edmonds 4–6) **and 139** (I. T. Botham 8–34). **England won by an innings and 120 runs.**

By the summer of 1978, Kerry Packer's World Series Cricket had completed its first season and the national teams decided to present a united front. England and Pakistan, who faced each other in 1978, adopted a hard line and suspended their Packer players. England lost Amiss, Greig, Knott, Snow, Underwood and Woolmer; only Knott and Underwood would play for England again. Pakistan dispensed with six men: Asif Iqbal, Imran Khan, Majid Khan, Mushtaq Mohammad, Sarfraz Nawaz and Zaheer Abbas; all would later return to the national fold, but it wrecked their tour of England.

Their weak side and the wet weather gave them a miserable time; their solitary win in two and a half months was in a two-day game against Surrey, who had already beaten them in Intikhab Alam's benefit match at Guildford. The first eight tour games were drawn, most after prolonged rain. Essex rolled them for 80, then England bundled them out for 85 in the first one-day international. By the end of the one-day series, they had four half-centuries to show for 10 games – and Mudassar Nazar had scored three of them.

Pakistan could hardly have been in a worse state going into the first Test at Birmingham – and they barely competed. They reached 91 for 2 on the first day, only to collapse hideously against Old, whose 7 for 50 included four wickets in five balls. Had last man Liaqat Ali not hung around for the best part of an hour, they would have made even fewer than 164. England took the lead on the second day for the loss of only two wickets. Clive Radley scored 106, and David Gower made 58, having pulled his first ball in Test cricket, from Liaqat, to the boundary. They only lost one more wicket that day (Gower) and batted most of the third as well. Botham reached his fifty from 89 balls, and his century from 135 – seriously quick in those days. England declared at 452, a lead of 288. There was no Underwood to terrorise Pakistan, but Edmonds took 4 for 44 as Pakistan lost by an innings, despite Sadiq Mohammad's 79.

First day – 15 June

During the seventies, the Queen increasingly came to the first day of the Test. Unfortunately, this year the rain prevented any play at all, but instead of inviting the Pakistanis to Buckingham Palace that evening, she came to Lord's anyway, and met the teams during the tea interval. The Test got underway on the second morning, and was a great one for Botham, who scored 108 and took 8 for 34 in the second innings.

After a day of rain, England got off to a stuttering start on the Friday morning, when Liaqat dismissed Brearley and Radley before the score had reached 20. But Gooch, with the first of his 66 Test half-centuries, and Gower, with the second of his 57, steadied the ship with a stand of 101. It wobbled again when both departed at 120, and Geoff Miller was out with the score on 134, but then came another hundred partnership, between Graham Roope and Botham. Roope played the accumulator role, while Botham smashed an explosive 108 from 110 balls. England were 308 for 8 at the end of the day, and though Botham went early on the third morning, his positive approach proved so contagious that Edmonds and Willis put on 40 for the last wicket.

Willis tore into Pakistan's top order, reducing them to 41 for 4, and though they recovered a little, Edmonds – in an eight-over spell which yielded only two scoring shots – triggered a collapse which saw the last six wickets fall for 21. By the close, Pakistan were 96 for 2 in the follow-on, Sadiq having edged Willis for the second time in the day. Then came the rest day – and it was a good job the Queen hadn't planned to come on the Monday afternoon, since the match would have been over. Botham took seven of the eight wickets to fall in the morning, including a final burst of 6 for 8. It was the best bowling performance of his entire Test career.

Pakistan fought their way back into contention at The Oval, but the weather was against them from the outset. Thanks to the conditions, their first innings of 201 spanned four days. England were 106 for 5 when the final day began, but it didn't last long; there was just enough time for Sarfraz Nawaz to complete a five-wicket haul before play was abandoned. After a consolation win against the Netherlands on their way home, Pakistan decided to put cricket before politics and forgave their Packerites. When India arrived for a tour in October, the prodigal six were back – and Pakistan won the series.

Another World Cup

London, 1979

The Queen was at Balmoral when the New Zealand team came to Lord's to begin their Test series in the second half of 1978. The Kiwis were completely unaffected by World Series Cricket – only Richard Hadlee had signed up, and he was allowed to join the touring party anyway – but were whitewashed in a three-match rubber.

The following year, India's Test tour of England was preceded by the second men's World Cup. Once again, the Queen held a reception on the eve of the opening games, at which she met the Canada team for the first time. But the late-summer scheduling of the Tests meant she was at Balmoral when the second Test began at Lord's, and by the time it concluded, she was sailing from Cowes on the Royal Yacht Britannia. She might just have made it in time to watch Dilip Vengsarkar and Viswanath complete their final-day centuries, but she was busy at the Palace, meeting her Ambassadors to Hungary, Algeria, Yemen and Greece. Having lost the first Test, India drew the next three; it was so rainy that they even dropped a spinner, going in with only two.

On 25 March 1980, Brearley became the fourth England captain to receive a personal invitation to Buckingham Palace. Invited to lunch alongside hm were Sir Geoffrey Chandler, an early champion of corporate social responsibility; Dr Kurt Hellmann, a prominent cancer researcher; David Lane, the chairman of the Commission for Racial Equality; the criminologist Sir Leon Radzinowicz; Commander Doug Taylor, who invented the "ski jump" runway for launching jets from aircraft carriers; and Ted Hughes, the Poet Laureate. Of all the England captains who were asked to attend such occasions, Brearley – later a psychoanalyst – must have held his own better than any.

delaide, March 1954. During her visit to Australia, the Queen watched a country cricket match. was the only time she met Sir Don Bradman, though he didn't play. [Hulton Archive/Getty]

Highclere, August 1958. The Duke of Edinburgh was a great cricket fan, and played as often as he ould. The Queen was a happy spectator on those occasions. [Hulton Archive/Getty]

Lord's, July 1975. Ian Chappell, captain of Australia, introduces the Queen to Max Walker in the second Ashes Test of the summer. The match was drawn. [Hulton Archive/Getty]

Melbourne, March 1977. Greg Chappell, who succeeded his brother Ian as captain, tries to stop England's Derek Randall (right) taking a quick single during his 174 in the Centenary Test. [Hulton Archive/Getty]

Lord's, June 1980. Andy Roberts, one of the great West Indies pacemen watched by the Queen during their days of dominance, went wicketless in the second Test. [Adrian Murrell/Allsport]

Lord's, June 1985. The MCC administrators seem to be having difficulty rolling out the red carpet for the Queen's visit. This was the only Test England lost during the Ashes series. [Adrian Murrell/Getty]

Lord's, June 1993. Shane Warne took eight wickets in the Ashes Test of 1993. [Ben Radford/Allsport]

Lord's, June 1999. Steve Waugh captained Australia to their World Cup final win. [AFP/Getty]

Lord's, July 2001. Glenn McGrath celebrates the dismissal of Mike Atherton. [Laurence Griffiths/Allsport]

Lord's, July 2001. Brett Lee was soon to become the world's fastest bowler. [Craig Prentis/Allsport]

oughborough, November 2003. The Queen and Prince Philip opened the ECB's new high
erformance academy, and were shown the ropes by Geoffrey Boycott. [Harry How/Getty]

uckingham Palace, February 2006. England's women had beaten Australia in a Test series for the first
me in 42 years, and were guests of honour – as were the men. [Fiona Hansen/AFP/Getty]

Lord's, May 2007. The Queen watching England play West Indies. She was such a regular, she provide little distraction from the Daily Mail. Neither did the cricket, in this case. [Tom Shaw/Getty]

Lord's, July 2004. Andrew Strauss of Middlesex scores his second Test century, in his debut season for England, and expresses his gratitude to his home ground. [Mike Hewitt/Getty]

Lord's, July 2004. Rob Key made 221 in the same innings, his final Test hundred. [Mike Hewitt/Getty]

Lord's, May 2007. Alastair Cook makes his fifth Test century, against West Indies. [Tom Shaw/Getty]

Lord's, July 2009. Not everyone maintained dignity in front of the Queen. Ricky Ponting expresses his displeasure at being given out, caught at slip, during the second Ashes Test. [Ian Kington/AFP/Getty]

Lord's, July 2013. The Queen leaves the field during her final visit to a cricket match. England won the second Test handsomely, and went on to retain the Ashes. [Anthony Devlin/WPA/Getty]

The Oval, September 2022. England and South Africa join a capacity crowd of 27,500 standing in silent tribute to the Queen, who died on the opening day of the Test. [Mike Hewitt, Getty]

Half an hour of Holding

England v West Indies at Lord's, 1980

England 269 (G. A. Gooch 123; M. A. Holding 6–67, C. E. G. Croft 4–36) **and 133 for 2. West Indies 518** (D. L. Haynes 184, I. V. A. Richards 145, C. H. Lloyd 56). **Drawn.**

West Indies were on the cusp of greatness – but there had been hiccups in getting there. Defections to World Series Cricket had cost them dear in 1978/79 when, in the absence of Greenidge, Haynes, Richards, Lloyd, Rowe, King and Murray, plus their all-conquering pace bowlers Croft, Garner, Holding and Roberts, they were obliged to send a de facto second eleven to India, and lost the series. The tour to New Zealand in 1979/80 was similarly fraught, as dodgy local umpiring and a lack of composure condemned them to another series defeat. Suffice to say that they were intent on proving a point when they arrived in England in May 1980. The missing eleven were all back, and were further strengthened by Alvin Kallicharran, who had captained West Indies in India, plus Faoud Bacchus and Malcolm Marshall, who had made promising debuts while the stars were away. Though Rowe's tour was cut short by a dislocated shoulder, the remaining 13 put England to the sword. Only two of their 28 games were lost all summer.

The West Indians made new friends and fans everywhere they went. Greenidge hit a century at Leicester, Lloyd against Northampton, Richards against Northampton and Essex. Marshall took 7 for 56 at Worcester, Garner 5 for 22 at Leicester, Holding 5 for 57 at Leicester. Greenidge's 78 won the first one-day international, though England sneaked home in the second. And, of course, it rained continually.

The first Test at Nottingham was a thrilling contest. England again found Roberts a handful, but his 5 for 72 could not stop them posting a respectable 263, with Botham – now captain – hitting 57. West Indies were kept within range, the visitors securing a lead of 45 after fifties from Greenidge, Richards and Murray. England made a great start to their second innings, reaching 174 for 2 before a dramatic collapse: they were all out for 252, of which Boycott made 75 in nearly six hours. Garner's extraordinary figures were 34.1–20–30–4. West Indies needed 208 to win, and by the close of the fourth day they required only 99 more, with eight wickets in hand. Barely 1,000 spectators turned up to watch the fifth day, but were rewarded by a rampant Willis, whose 5 for 65 reduced West Indies to 180 for 7. But Roberts was dropped, and the visitors made it over the line.

West Indies rotated their seamers for the Lord's Test, which the Queen was due to visit on the Monday after the rest day. Rain and bad light blighted the game, but the tourists nonetheless worked themselves into a position of dominance. Gooch's first-day 123 was fierce, but Holding – who took 6 for 67 – shared all 10 wickets with Garner, and by the close of the second day, West Indies were 265 for 2, just four behind England's total. Richards hit a terrific 145 off 159 balls, and though England bowled well, they looked like boys against men – or men against giants. There was little let-up on the Saturday, as Lloyd's half-century helped Haynes reach 184, the biggest of his 18 Test hundreds. West Indies were all out for 518, a lead of 249. England had reached 33 for 0 by the rest day.

Fourth day – 23 June

The Queen reverted to her original custom of visiting Lord's on day four: the Monday after the rest day. Fate again conspired to deny her a decent cricketing spectacle. Had she come on the first day, she would have seen Graham Gooch's maiden Test century. England began the Monday on 33 for 0 in their second innings. In the half hour's play that was possible before lunch, they reached 51 for 0; it rained for the rest of the day, and the Queen met the teams in the pavilion.

Even compared with the Queen's typical misfortunes as a cricket-watcher, the Monday of the Lord's Test was awful. Half an hour's play was possible, during which Gooch and Boycott added 17 runs while Holding worked up pace and bounce; the rain set in before lunch, and the rest of the day was washed out. Under such circumstances, the Queen would usually have invited the West Indians to the Palace that evening, but on this occasion she went to Lord's, where Knott met her for the 11th time, passing Cowdrey and Barrington's record.

Rain also ruined the third Test at Manchester, where England battled hard after Lloyd's century had given West Indies a lead of 110. They fought at The Oval, too: at 92 for 9 in their second innings, they had a lead of 197 – and Peter Willey's century, in a last-wicket rearguard of 117 with Willis, saved the game. The fifth Test at Leeds was another damp draw. Still, West Indies won the series; they would not lose another until May 1995.

The calm before the storm

England v Australia at Lord's, 1981

England 311 (P. Willey 82, M. W. Gatting 59; G. F. Lawson 7–81) **and
265 for 8 declared** (D. I. Gower 89, G. Boycott 60). **Australia 345**
(A. R. Border 64) **and 90 for 4** (G. M. Wood 62*). **Drawn.**

It was six years since Australia had held the Ashes and, having
received a 5–1 hiding at home in 1978/79, they were faced with
a tricky tour in 1981, as they rebuilt in the post-Packer era. Greg
Chappell, vilified in February for the underarm bowling controversy
at Melbourne, decided not to tour, and Kim Hughes, who had
often led Australia when the big boys were playing World Series
Cricket, was appointed captain in his place. This bothered Lillee,
who felt Marsh should lead the side, and it was a fractious squad
that set off around the counties in May. An ignominious defeat
to the Duchess of Norfolk's XI, which saw Australia bowled out
for 106, kicked off the tour. Four draws, inevitably wet, followed
against the counties; no one scored a century, and no one took
five wickets. Lillee had pneumonia and couldn't play. It was
therefore something of a shock that Australia won the one-day
international series, especially after losing the first match. Lillee
made his comeback, leading the attack, and Graeme Wood made
a century in the third game. There was a positive mood as the first
Test approached – but most of the tourists were still desperately
short of runs. Mike Brearley outscored them all with a princely 132
not out in their tour match against Middlesex.

Fortunately for Australia, England came unstuck with the bat at
Nottingham. Terry Alderman, on his international debut, caused
them unending bother with 4 for 68 and 5 for 62, dismissing Boycott
twice. There was only one half-century on each side: Gatting's 52
and Allan Border's 63. Australia prevailed in a low-scoring tussle by
tiptoeing to a target of 132. It was an inauspicious start for Botham's
England. Australia played out two sodden draws with Lancashire
and Kent before the second Test at Lord's.

First day – 2 July

The Queen attended on the first day, which was affected by bad light. The dominant force was Geoff Lawson who, having never previously taken more than two wickets in a Test innings, returned first-innings figures of 7 for 81. He took the first three wickets to fall and sent Bob Woolmer packing with a bruised arm.

The Lord's Test of 1981 included a Sunday rest day, even though the previous Test at Trent Bridge had been the first in England to feature Sunday play. The Queen attended the first day for a change, but her luck stayed the same. England crawled to 191 for 4 in murky conditions before bad light stopped play: Gooch hit a typically robust 44 and was first to go with the score on 60; Boycott, who had drawn level with Knott in meeting the Queen an 11th time, plodded to 17 in an hour and 40 minutes and was next out at 65. Woolmer retired hurt at 83, having been hit on the arm by Lawson, but Gower added 51 with Gatting before being caught behind off Marsh (who equalled Walters's Australian record of meeting the Queen six times). Gatting and Willey rallied, though Gatting was out for 59 just before play was abandoned for the day; Emburey came in as nightwatchman.

Play didn't restart until the second afternoon, when Willey and Emburey steered England to 284 for 4. But Lawson, irresistible, then swept the hosts away – including Botham, for a duck – to finish with 7 for 81, easily his best Test figures. England were all out for 311. Australia's innings followed a reverse pattern: they were struggling at 81 for 4, but doughty resistance, led by Border's 64, gave them a lead of 34. England did their best to set a tough target: after Boycott and Gower had laid the foundation with careful half-centuries, the middle order hit out. Botham was lbw first ball to Ray Bright, completing a pair, and Australia were set 232 in just under three hours. Though they fell to 17 for 3, the draw was secured easily enough.

Botham quit the captaincy following the match and advocated for Brearley's return. The change sparked a stunning turnaround in fortunes. His 149 not out, and Willis's iconic 8 for 43, brought England victory after following on at Leeds. His spell of 5 for 1 halted Australia's cruise to a target of 151 at Birmingham. And his outrageous 118 from 102 balls put England in a match-winning position at Manchester. England had now won three successive Ashes series for the first time since 1956, and only the second time in the 20th century. By the time Botham reached The Oval for the sixth Test, he was exhausted, but still managed to bowl 89 overs in the match, claiming 10 wickets. 'Botham's Ashes' brought him 399 runs at 36, and 34 wickets at 20. Rarely had a player dominated a Test series so emphatically. Brearley, the captain who had brought the best out of him, immediately retired from international cricket.

A record for Randall

England v India at Lord's, 1982

England 433 (D. W. Randall 126, I. T. Botham 67, P. H. Edmonds 64; Kapil Dev 5–125) **and 67 for 3**. **India 128** (I. T. Botham 5–46) **and 369** (D. B. Vengsarkar 157, Kapil Dev 89; R. G. D. Willis 6–101). **England won by seven wickets.**

England experienced quite a comedown after the thrills of the 1981 Ashes. A long tour of India, stretching from November until February, sapped their energy and patience. They lost the first Test in Mumbai and the remaining five matches were drawn. There was a consolation win for England in Colombo, where they played Sri Lanka for the first time, but they returned home haunted by Sunil Gavaskar, who faced 1,382 balls for 500 runs – still the most by any Indian in a Test series. He would hurt England again when India visited for a three-match series in 1982, sharing the summer with Pakistan.

England, with Willis as their new captain, hoped for green pitches and overcast conditions, but India felt they could counter them well enough given the success of their own seamers in the home series win. The Duchess of Norfolk's XI vanquished another touring team, despite the age of their players (Robin Hobbs played at 39, John Snow and John Jameson at 40, and Tony Lewis at 43) – by 10 wickets this time, as Andy Stovold and Sadiq Mohammad chased down a target of 202. But the Indians grew in confidence, not least Gavaskar, who hit a remarkable 172 after lunch on the final day against Warwickshire. England won both one-day internationals, with Allan Lamb making 99 at The Oval.

The first Test began with a wonderful display of swing bowling from Kapil Dev, who reduced England to 96 for 4. Botham, at number five, smashed an assertive half-century, but when he and Derek Pringle were out in quick succession, England were 166 for 6 and in a pickle. It fell to Randall, back in the Test team after two and a half years in the wilderness, to mastermind a recovery.

He was well into a seventh-wicket stand of 125 with Edmonds when stumps were drawn.

Second day – 11 June

On the second day, Derek Randall became the first cricketer to score two hundreds in front of the Queen, and Kapil Dev completed figures of 5 for 125. Gundappa Viswanath matched Bishan Bedi's Indian record, set at the World Cup reception in 1979, by meeting the Queen for a fourth time. It was the last time the Queen saw a match involving India.

Randall's 126 spanned nearly six hours and lifted England to 433, despite Kapil Dev's 5 for 125. Edmonds extended his highest Test score to 64, then Taylor made 31, Paul Allott an unbeaten 41 – and even Willis made 28. Then, late in the day, England made inroads on a pitch now offering uneven bounce. Botham trapped Ghulam Parkar in front, Willis did the same to Vengsarkar, Botham bowled Viswanath, then Pringle had Yashpal Sharma and Ashok Malhotra lbw. At the close, India were 92 for 5, with Gavaskar clinging on.

He didn't last much longer on the Saturday and Botham completed a haul of 5 for 46 as India capitulated for 128 and followed on, 305 behind. They were 61 for 2 when the rest day came, with Parkar and Gavaskar the men dismissed. Vengsarkar set out to bat the whole of Monday, and played a dogged innings of 157; when he was out, Kapil Dev smashed an outrageous 89 off 55 balls to bring India past 300 and set the hosts a target. Willis had taken 6 for 101. England only needed 65, but a burst from Kapil Dev reduced them to 23 for 3 at the close. Within an hour on the fifth day, they had secured victory.

The Manchester Test was drawn, but only after Botham had made an aggressive 128, setting up an England total of 425, and Sharma had smashed Willis for 24 off an over, equalling the Test record. Sandeep Patil's unbeaten 129 brought India to 379 for 8 before rain washed out the final day. The third Test, on a flat batting pitch at The Oval, saw another world record. England were already sitting pretty at 185 for 3 when Botham came to the wicket, and he hammered home their advantage; he hit his fourth ball so hard at Gavaskar that it broke his leg. Adding 176 with Lamb, who made a hundred, and 151 with Randall, who fell five short of his, Botham walloped 208 off 226 balls, the fastest double-century in international cricket. Kapil Dev then plundered 97 off 93 in a high-scoring draw. England thus won the series, and though Pakistan played a Test at Lord's in August, the Queen was taking her annual holiday at Balmoral.

And another World Cup

London, 1983

For the third time in succession, England hosted the men's World Cup. And for the third time, the Queen hosted a reception on the eve of the opening game. The tournament included a first appearance for Zimbabwe, a team she never saw play, though she at least met Duncan Fletcher's squad at the Palace. Several cricketers set their national records for most meetings with the Queen: Turner for New Zealand (five times), Lloyd for West Indies and Wasim Bari for Pakistan (six times), and Marsh for Australia (seven times).

The competition itself was famous for India's surprise win in the final. Though their victory didn't end the West Indies' domination of world cricket, it sowed the seed for India's later primacy. England, losing semi-finalists in 1975 and runners-up in 1979, also fell victim to India, in the semis. England played a four-Test series against New Zealand following the World Cup, which they won 3–1 after New Zealand had levelled the series at Leeds. Lord's hosted the third Test; Gower scored a century and debutant Nick Cook took a five-wicket haul to put England ahead again.

The Queen, once again, was dividing her time between Balmoral and the Britannia. She did not put in an appearance at Lord's in 1984 – her third fallow year, after 1970 and 1974 – and thus missed the sensational Lord's Test in which Greenidge's unbeaten 214 powered West Indies to a fifth-day target of 342 (she was on the way to Balmoral as he did it). She was in Scotland again when Sri Lanka came to Lord's in August, and England – now captained by Gower – earned a draw after being whitewashed by West Indies. There was one notable Royal cricketing moment in 1984, though: HRH Princess Anne, who had attended the first women's World Cup final in 1973, attended the third women's one-day international between England and New Zealand, in Bristol. England won by 55 runs after Jan Brittin and Jan Allen's opening stand of 152.

Swinging in the rain

England v Australia at Lord's, 1985

England 290 (D. I. Gower 86; C. J. McDermott 6–70) **and 261** (I. T. Botham 85, M. W. Gatting 75; R. G. Holland 5–68). **Australia 425** (A. R. Border 196, G. M. Ritchie 94; I. T. Botham 5–109) **and 127 for 6.**
Australia won by four wickets.

It was Australia's turn to receive a beating from West Indies in 1984/85. Malcolm Marshall was all over them, taking five wickets in an innings four times, but the Aussies did at least win a Test, in the dead rubber at Sydney. It suggested they might be more than a match for England, not least because they had regained the Ashes at home in 1982/83.

For the 1985 Ashes, England were led by Gower, who had captained them to an attritional series win in India; Border skippered Australia on the tour, as he had against West Indies. He scored three centuries in the pre-Ashes county games; in the first, at Taunton, Thomson rediscovered his zip of old, taking 6 for 44 in the second innings. David Boon, Greg Ritchie, Simon O'Donnell, Wayne Phillips and Graeme Wood added hundreds of their own – and Australia won the one-day series. Their batters were thus in prime form going into the Tests – but their bowling was a worry. Apart from Thomson, none of the seamers had fired; it was a problem that would haunt them all summer.

Australia did well enough to score 331 in the first innings of the Leeds Test – Andrew Hilditch made 119 and 80 in the game – but their bowling attack had the cutting edge of wet tissue paper. Tim Robinson, England's new opener, scored 175, helping the hosts to a lead of 202. Australia's 324 in the second innings was respectable enough, especially as the pitch was starting to turn, Emburey taking 5 for 82, but it posed no great challenge to England, who scythed their way to the target of 123. Botham had been in ominous form, smashing 60 off 51 in the first innings and taking seven wickets in the match. Australia had only a low-key game against Oxford and

107

Cambridge Universities and a damp one against Hampshire before the second Test.

Border won a good toss at Lord's. He knew the pitch would be slow and offer turn for Bob Holland, his leg-spinner, and he gambled on his three seamers being able to bowl England out for a manageable total. Craig McDermott found plenty of lateral movement, and had the openers, Gooch and Robinson, lbw before Lawson removed Gatting in the same fashion before 100 was up. Gower stroked a fluent 86 but was fourth out, to McDermott with the score on 179, and Lawson soon removed Botham and Lamb. Paul Downton became McDermott's fourth victim, and O'Donnell trapped Emburey in front after a typically idiosyncratic 33. England were 273 for 8 at the close, with only the tail left.

Second day – 28 June

Once again, the Queen's visit to Lord's coincided with bad weather; there were five rain breaks, between which the seamers flourished. Craig McDermott completed a haul of 6 for 70, and Australia struggled to 101 for 4 before Allan Border mastered the bowling, setting off on his way to a match-winning 196.

The Queen's jinx showed no sign of abating. Play was interrupted five times on the second day, before bad light eventually ended it early. The overhead conditions were ideal for swing, and McDermott quickly toppled Edmonds and Neil Foster, finishing with 6 for 70, the best figures of his Test career to date. But England found swing too: Paul Allott had Wood caught, Foster bowled Hilditch, and Botham got Kepler Wessels and Boon. Australia were teetering at 101 for 4, but Border took control. He batted with assertiveness and flair, finding a capable partner in Ritchie, with whom he added 82 by stumps.

They batted until after lunch on the third day, by which time Australia were past England. Ritchie did not reach his century, being pinned lbw by Botham, but the stand was worth 216 and guaranteed the visitors a healthy lead. Border's 196 was his highest score in Tests to that point, and though Botham took 5 for 109, England were still staring at a deficit of 135. They had lost both openers by the rest day, and things went from bad to worse on Monday morning, when McDermott and Lawson reduced them to 98 for 6. Botham, coming in at eight, did his best to arrest the decline by attacking. It worked for a while – he thrashed 85 off 117 – and Edmonds clung on, facing 34 balls for 1, but Holland's 5 for 68 meant Australia only needed 127. They wobbled, but Border's unbeaten 41 made sure of victory.

There were run-heavy draws at Nottingham and Manchester, marked by hundreds for Gower, Wood, Ritchie, Gatting and Border; McDermott's 8 for 141 in England's innings of 482 at Old Trafford was an impressive feat of stamina. The teams reached The Oval with the series all square, but it was England who prevailed. They plundered 595 for 5, with Gower making 215, and Richard Ellison took a match haul of 10 for 94 to win the Ashes for the fourth series in five.

Is there a keeper in the house?

England v New Zealand at Lord's, 1986

England 307 (M. D. Moxon 74, D. I. Gower 62; R. J. Hadlee 6–80) **and 295 for 6 declared** (G. A. Gooch 183). **New Zealand 342** (M. D. Crowe 106, B. A. Edgar 83, J. V. Coney 51; G. R. Dilley 4–82, P. H. Edmonds 4–97) **and 41 for 2. Drawn.**

Having won the World Cup on their previous visit to England, three years earlier, India felt confident ahead of their early-summer Tests – and their optimism was fully justified, as they won comfortably at Lord's and Leeds to claim the series.

The Queen did not come to Lord's for the India game, choosing instead to watch New Zealand, who were England's opponents in the second half of the season. She had not seen the Kiwis on the field since 1969, and they were now a different proposition altogether. Indeed, Jeremy Coney's team were arguably now better than England; they had beaten Australia in 1985/86 and had several world-class players, including the formidable fast bowler Richard Hadlee. England gave a debut to Martyn Moxon, and he grabbed his opportunity, scoring 74 out of the hosts' first-day total of 248 for 5. Gower, who had passed on the captaincy to Gatting, made 62. New Zealand had a peculiarly unbalanced bowling group. At one end, they had Hadlee, bustling in with pace, swing and relentless accuracy. At the other, they circulated five bowlers who, even on their best days, were no better than a county attack. Their best chances lay in hoping for a mistake.

Second day – 25 July

Richard Hadlee, who met the Queen for a fifth time, equalling Glenn Turner's New Zealand record, completed a superb haul of 6 for 80 as England were dismissed for 307. An injury to

Bruce French meant England had no wicketkeeper. Jeremy Coney, the visiting captain, allowed them to call on the services of Bob Taylor, by then retired and working for the match sponsor. By the close, Martin Crowe had got halfway to the majestic hundred he completed the following day. It was the last time the Queen attended a match involving New Zealand.

On the second morning, Hadlee worked his way through England's lower order, finishing with 6 for 80. There was a horrible moment when Bruce French, England's wicketkeeper, turned his back on a Hadlee bouncer and was struck on the back of the helmet. He required three stitches, was badly concussed, and left England with a headache, too: who would keep wicket? Word went round the ground that Taylor – by then 45 and working for Cornhill Insurance, the match's sponsor – was in a hospitality tent. Generously, Coney agreed that he could don the gloves as a substitute (the laws did not permit this unless the opposing captain gave permission). Bill Athey kept for two overs while Taylor got changed, and then the veteran put on a nimble, competent display until Bobby Parks, the Sussex gloveman, made it to Lord's.

New Zealand quickly lost John Wright and Ken Rutherford for ducks to Dilley but recovered through Bruce Edgar and Martin Crowe's partnership of 200, which stretched into the third day. Edgar didn't make it to a century, being dismissed by Gooch for 83, but Crowe played with characteristic elegance for 106. Edmonds whirled away, removing Crowe and his brother, Jeff. Neal Radford dismissed Coney for 51, then Edmonds and Dilley shared the tailenders between them. New Zealand had batted all day, eking out a small but precious lead of 35. But after the rest day, the rain came. England pottered to 110 for 3 when conditions allowed – Moxon, Athey and Gower all failed – but their slow progress ruled out a result on the final day. Gooch struck a commanding 183 as England batted out most of the remaining overs; there was just enough time for a declaration and 15 overs in the field – Wright completed a pair – before the captains shook hands on a draw.

The second Test at Nottingham went right down to the wire, with New Zealand trying to bowl England out on the fifth day in time to chase a target. They had won the toss and put England in, and the decision seemed to have been justified when England managed a modest 256. Hadlee took 6 for 80 as England struggled to master him. New Zealand slipped to 144 for 5, but were rescued, first by Hadlee's 68, then by John Bracewell's resolute 110 at number eight. England were 157 behind and could only set the visitors 74, which they got with eight overs to spare. A draw at The Oval gave New Zealand their first series victory in England at the 10th attempt.

An audience with Aboriginals

London, 1988

The Queen had no cricketing engagements in 1987 – the fourth year of her reign without them – which was probably just as well, since the Lord's Test against Pakistan was reduced to less than 113 overs by rain. A unique occasion made up for it the following year. In recognition of the 120 years that had passed since an Aboriginal team visited England, the Australian government sent a squad of indigenous cricketers to the UK to play 29 games against counties, amateur clubs and invitation XIs.

Surrey, Kent, Sussex, Hampshire, Glamorgan and Lancashire hosted the visitors, who gave a good account of themselves, and they were received at Buckingham Palace on 21 June. Such a joyous occasion was a tonic to the cricketing turmoil of 1988. After their acrimonious tour of Pakistan, England were thrashed by West Indies, going through four captains in the process: Gatting, Emburey, Chris Cowdrey and Gooch. Cries to reform the County Championship, to rid it of a surfeit of three-day games, with their contrived declarations, were growing louder. And India announced that they would not allow England to visit while their squad contained men who had participated in the rebel tour to South Africa in 1981/82 (a problem which would be compounded by the organisation of another rebel tour, in 1989/90).

The Queen missed both Lord's Tests of 1988; West Indies won in June, with Marshall claiming 10 for 92 and Greenidge scoring a crucial second-innings 103; despite a counterattacking 113 from Lamb, England fell well short of their target of 442. At the end of August, Sri Lanka visited again, and were comfortably beaten after falling to 63 for 6 on the first day. Though Sri Lanka was a Commonwealth country, the Queen never saw them play cricket. In all likelihood, the Palace received advice from the English cricket authorities, who wanted her to see a great occasion. A full stadium at Lord's against the mighty Australia or West Indies would no doubt have been suitable – but, in those days, English cricket had little interest in sporting minnows, and the home board probably deemed Sri Lanka an inferior spectacle. It would be another 10 years before that assumption was turned squarely on its head.

A comeback after Anything Goes

England v Australia at Lord's, 1989

England 286 (R. C. Russell 64*, G. A. Gooch 60, D. I. Gower 57; M. G. Hughes 4–71) **and 359** (D. I. Gower 106, R. A. Smith 96; T. M. Alderman 6–128). **Australia 528** (S. R. Waugh 152*, D. C. Boon 94, G. F. Lawson 74, M. A. Taylor 62; J. E. Emburey 4–88) **and 119 for 4** (D. C. Boon 58*).
Australia won by six wickets.

England's decline continued apace. The 1989 Ashes was the start of an era of near-total Australian dominance which lasted until the next century. Chastened by the defeats of 1985 and 1986/87, Australian captain Allan Border resolved to battle-harden his men. There was to be no quarter given on the field – not even smiles. His team were going to war, and they were going to win. Creating a winning habit, and an aura of invincibility, Border felt, would be the key to long-term success. Australia battered two invitation teams at the start of the tour, lost a one-day game to Sussex, then destroyed the MCC after David Boon and Geoff Marsh shared an opening partnership of 277. They lost to Worcestershire after Phil Newport took 11 wickets, ensuring his selection for England, but beat Middlesex, Yorkshire and Derbyshire, as well as drawing the one-day international series.

When it came to the Ashes, Australia were in dominant mood. England made mistake upon mistake, starting in the first Test at Leeds, where Gower – now back in the captain's chair – invited Australia to bat first. They made 601, with Mark Taylor scoring 136 at the top of the order, and Steve Waugh making an unbeaten 177 at No. 6. They kept England in the field until the third day, but the hosts fought back gamely through a hundred from Lamb. With a lead of 171, Australia piled on the pressure, racing to 230 for 3 by the final morning, and giving themselves 83 overs to bowl England out. They needed only 55, as Alderman, aided by great catching in the slips, took 5 for 44. The pattern of the series had been set.

On winning the toss at Lord's, Gower managed not to make the same mistake twice, but even so, England's batters could not last the day. Alderman was again incisive, and Merv Hughes bowled with aggression to bowl the hosts out for 286. Gooch, Gower and Jack Russell made half-centuries, but could not go on. By the end of the second day, Australia were only 10 runs behind England, with four wickets in hand. Boon had played well for 94, but the bowlers had plugged away, and would be in the game if they could finish Australia off quickly on Saturday morning. But they couldn't – far from it. Australia batted most of the day, scoring another 252 runs, most of them from the bat of Waugh, who remained unbeaten with 152. Facing an uphill task, 242 behind on first innings, England wobbled to 58 for 3 by close. Gower, not in the best of moods – and with tickets to see *Anything Goes* that evening – walked out of the post-play press conference.

Fourth day – 26 June

England were still 184 behind, with seven wickets in hand, when they began the day. David Gower and Robin Smith battled hard, adding 139 and pushing England towards a lead. Terry Alderman was relentless, finishing with 6 for 128, but Gower's 106 and Smith's 96 gave the home crowd something to cheer.

Gower was censured for his behaviour in the press conference, but more than made amends for it on the Monday. England were expected to capitulate early, and Gatting was lbw to Alderman at 84, but Gower and Robin Smith knuckled down for four and a half hours, putting on 139. Gower's captain's innings of 106 showed fight and determination, but also his characteristic fluency and timing; it was ended when he gloved a Hughes lifter. Smith, who added 51 with Russell, looked like making his first Test century, but was bowled by Alderman, four short. England were 80 ahead by the close, with the last pair together.

Dilley and Emburey extended the England lead to 117 on the final morning before a heavy thunderstorm threatened to deny Australia the chance to go 2–0 up. Play was possible from half past two, however, and though Australia, in their haste, slid to 67 for 4, Boon's second half-century of the match ensured there was no upset.

Wet weather ruled out any chance of a result at Birmingham but, with six Tests scheduled, England still had hopes of an unlikely turnaround to save the Ashes – but they were dashed by the halfway stage at Manchester. Despite Smith's glorious 143, England managed only 260 batting first, with Lawson taking 6 for 72, and Australia were soon out of sight. Waugh top-scored with 92, and England were 187 behind on first innings. Then it was Alderman's turn to impress: he reduced England to 59 for 6 before Russell mounted a rearguard action with Emburey, which took the game to the last day. Russell's unbeaten 128 was his maiden first-class century but it could not prevent Australia from regaining the Ashes with a nine-wicket win. They won again at Nottingham, where Gower asked them to bat first, only for the tourists to cruise to 301 for 0 by the end of the first day. Utterly crushed, England lost by an innings, and would surely have lost at The Oval too had rain not ruined a day's worth of play.

Nine cricketing knights

Wellington, 1990

The Queen personally dubbed the first eight cricketers to be knighted during her reign. The first was Henry Leveson Gower, in early 1953; though he had played Test cricket, the honour was more for his service to the game. He was an England selector at various times between 1909 and 1930, and helped organise the Scarborough Festival for 50 years. Later that year, the Queen knighted Jack Hobbs. She had never seen him play – she was only eight when he retired – but he was undoubtedly the greatest living English cricketer when he was knighted at the age of 70. He had worked as a journalist, and written several books, but was a modest man, and did not like the thought that he was the first professional cricketer to be knighted. He only accepted when convinced the honour represented all working cricketers, not just himself.

Four outstanding cricketing figures, with very different roles, were next to be knighted. Len Hutton was England's pre-eminent post-War batter, scoring 6,971 test runs at an average of 56, and 40,140 runs in first-class cricket. His England career spanned the Second World War – 18 years in total – and he captained the national team 23 times. He was knighted in 1956. Learie Constantine was honoured six years later. Of him, more hereafter. Frank Worrell was the first of the West Indies' famous three Ws to be knighted, receiving the honour in 1964, the year after his retirement. Neville Cardus, arguably the greatest cricket writer of the 20th century, received a knighthood in 1967.

After Sobers was knighted in Barbados, Gubby Allen was next to receive the honour, in 1986. He had been perhaps English cricket's most influential administrator, and was a champion of professional and state-educated cricketers who sought to experience the privileges usually reserved for the higher classes. He served as an England selector, was on the MCC committee, and was instrumental in setting up English cricket's first truly independent cricket board, the Cricket Council, which was a forerunner of the ECB.

But The Queen did not personally dub her ninth cricketing knight. Richard Hadlee learned of his knighthood on 16 June 1990, when New Zealand were playing a tour match at Northampton. Five days later, the Lord's Test began, and though the Queen did not attend, Hadlee received an ovation. He had become the leading wicket-taker in international cricket, but since he did not receive his knighthood until after his retirement – he was honoured on 4 October by the Governor General of New Zealand at Government House in Wellington – he narrowly missed playing professional cricket as Sir Richard Hadlee. The Queen watched no cricket in 1990; had she been at Lord's for the India Test, a 247-run win for England which included Gooch's 333, she would have seen one of the great games at headquarters.

A second trip across the river

The Oval, 1991

West Indies, having won the first Test of the 1991 series, had taken a first-innings lead of 65 in the second Test at Lord's, only for rain to wash out the fourth day which, this year, was a Sunday (there was no rest day). The Queen had intended to visit on Monday. But only 4.5 overs were possible, during which Phil Simmons and Richie Richardson were dismissed before the rain returned. For the first time since 1972, the Queen replaced her visit to Lord's with a reception at the Palace and on this occasion she invited both teams, something she had not done since 1954. Greenidge equalled Lloyd's West Indian record by meeting her for the sixth time.

The series was a classic, drawn 2–2 after England's exhilarating win, inspired by Phil Tufnell, at The Oval. The Queen visited the ground for only the second time since 1955, but not to watch the Test. Instead, she was there a week before the match, opening the Ken Barrington Centre, a state-of-the-art practice facility. While there, she saw Surrey play Essex in the quarter-final of the Nat West Trophy, her first professional limited-overs game (though she had seen one-day exhibition matches in 1954 at Adelaide, 1957 at Guildford and 1960 at Lord's). Surrey scored 253 and bowled Essex out for 222. Waqar Younis was in supreme form, triggering a collapse from 172 for 3. The Queen met both teams on the field, including Alec Stewart, the first cricketer whose father she had also seen play; she had seen Micky Stewart three times between 1955 and 1963. Sri Lanka visited Lord's for a Test at the end of August; Gooch set England up with a second-innings 174, and Tufnell's five wickets sealed victory.

Cowdrey at the Council

London, 1992

The International Cricket Council, as it is now known, has its roots in 1909, when representatives of England, Australia and South Africa formed the Imperial Cricket Conference. India, New Zealand and West Indies were added in 1926, and Pakistan in 1947. In the early sixties, the decision was taken to admit non-Test playing nations as associate members, and to restyle the organisation as the International Cricket Conference. The first associates were Fiji, Sri Lanka (then Ceylon) and the USA. But the organisation was still, for all intents and purposes, Anglocentric. The headquarters were in London – at Lord's – and there was a tradition that the President of MCC was automatically the Chairman of the ICC.

The English hegemony was broken in 1989 with the adoption of a new constitution, which created the International Cricket Council with an independent president. The first to take office was Colin Cowdrey, who held the post from 1989 to 1993. He had been President of MCC in 1986, so perhaps it was a case of *plus ça change, plus c'est la même chose*. It was announced that he was to be knighted in the New Year Honours of 1992; he received the honour on 10 March at Buckingham Palace. His successor at the ICC was Clyde Walcott, who was president from 1993 to 1997. He, too, was knighted during his tenure, by the government of Barbados, and in 1995, Everton Weekes became the last of the three Ws to be thus honoured.

Warne and May take their turn

England v Australia at Lord's, 1993

Australia 632 for 4 declared (D. C. Boon 164, M. J. Slater 152, M. A. Taylor 111, M. E. Waugh 99, A. R. Border 77). **England 205** (M. A. Atherton 80; M. G. Hughes 4–52, S. K. Warne 4–57) **and 365** (M. A. Atherton 99, G. A. Hick 64, A. J. Stewart 62, M. W. Gatting 59; T. B. A. May 4–81, S. K. Warne 4–102). **Australia won by an innings and 62 runs.**

The Queen had no cricketing engagements when Pakistan toured in 1992, which meant she went four years, between two Ashes series, without seeing an international game. In truth, it seemed her appetite for cricket wasn't what it was; whereas she used to watch one or two matches a year, now the Palace cherry-picked only the most auspicious occasions. On 20 April, Dexter became the fifth England captain to be personally invited to meet her, when he went to dinner at Windsor – the only cricketer to visit the Castle, other than Denness. Dexter was not, of course, there as a player, but in his capacity as chair of the England Cricket Committee.

England's rotation of captains had been arrested at the end of the eighties, and Gooch was now the incumbent. A successful one, too: as well as his captain's innings against India in 1990 and Sri Lanka in 1991, he had secured a drawn series with West Indies in 1991, and had taken England to their first World Cup final since 1979 (though the outcome was the same). A great battle lay ahead: his first home Ashes series in charge. Having lost in Australia in 1990/91, he was determined to show Border's team the same fight that had been shown against Richards' West Indians.

The 1993 Ashes began brightly enough for England. Australia's first innings at Manchester reacquainted the hosts with a now-customary thorn-in-the-side in the form of Taylor, who scored 124, but introduced a new English weapon, in the form of Essex off-spinner Peter Such. His 6 for 67, which helped dismiss Australia for a modest 289, was seen as a thrilling sign that the Ashes might just be won by spin. By the end of the second day, that possibility seemed even more likely – not through Such, but through Shane Warne, the prodigiously talented leg-spinner whose first delivery to Gatting would go down in legend. It dipped, pitched outside leg, then turned to clip off stump. Warne's 4 for 51 helped Australia to a lead of 79, and they never looked back. Ian Healy's unbeaten hundred set England 512, and once Gooch was out – handling a ball from Hughes which threatened to bounce onto his wicket – they soon subsided.

England stuck to their guns. For the second Test at Lord's, they made just one change, recalling Foster for his first Test in nearly four years (he had served a ban for joining the second rebel tour of South Africa) in place of Phil DeFreitas. As at Old Trafford, Gooch banked on Chris Lewis as a bowling all-rounder at number seven, two spinners in Such and Phil Tufnell, and Andy Caddick with the new ball. The strategy was not a success. Australia were 292 for 2 at the end of the first day, and added another 300 on the second, with centuries for Taylor, Michael Slater and Boon, and 99 for Mark Waugh. They declared at 632 for 6, and England began their reply in a state of shock. They made a paltry 205, despite the Australians missing McDermott, who was rushed to hospital with a twisted bowel and played no part in the match. The snarling aggression of Hughes, and spin pairing of Tim May and Warne, were more than enough. Michael Atherton stood apart, phlegmatically accumulating 80, and did even better in the follow-on, until he slipped mid-pitch going for his 100th run, and was run out. England were 237 for 3 at the start of the final day, still 190 short of making Australia bat again, but with a slim chance of saving the Test.

Fifth day – 21 June

Needing to bat out the day to save the game, England steadily lost their seven remaining wickets. Graeme Hick and Alec Stewart made half-centuries, but the Australian spinners could not be resisted for long, and the end came swiftly. From 304 for 4, England were all out for 365, with

Tim May and Shane Warne the chief destroyers. Graham Gooch joined Geoffrey Boycott and Alan Knott in meeting the Queen 11 times.

Save for the run-out of Atherton, all England's second-innings wickets fell to spin. Border dismissed Foster, May took four middle-order wickets, and Warne claimed four for the fourth innings in succession. He took three in each innings in the drawn third Test at Nottingham, in which Graham Thorpe made a century on debut and Caddick briefly gave England hope of winning when Australia fell to 115 for 6 on the final day. But Steve Waugh and Brendon Julian saved them, and Paul Reiffel bowled them to victory at Leeds (where Border made an unbeaten 200) and Birmingham, thus securing the Ashes. Gooch resigned the captaincy and, under Atherton, England claimed a consolation victory in a dead rubber at The Oval.

Back into the fold

Highclere, 1994

New Zealand played a series in England in the early summer of 1994, but it was merely an appetiser for the main event: the first visit of a South African team since 1965. Apartheid had come to an end, and South Africans looked to the future with hope. Though there were no non-white members of the touring party, other than assistant manager Goolam Rajah, this was a consequence of past actions rather than present decisions, and the recently elected deputy president of South Africa, Thabo Mbeki, was a beaming presence at Lord's for the first Test.

First, though, there were warm-up fixtures. Sir Paul Getty hosted a match at his private ground in Buckinghamshire, where the South Africans played among themselves, save for somewhat incongruous guest appearances by three recent retirees: Simon Hughes of Middlesex, Andy Lloyd of Warwickshire, and the irrepressible Randall. The official opening fixture was on 23 June at Highclere Castle – later known, on television at least, as Downton Abbey – against the Earl of Carnarvon's XI.

The Queen was present for the Earl's roll call of local and international talent against the tourists in a one-day game. Chris Broad, his England career over but still playing for Gloucestershire, was out early, but Gregor Macmillan laid a platform alongside Trevor Ward and Chris Adams. But, from 146 for 3, the Earl's team slowly subsided. Gower, the captain, was out for 7, and only enterprising hitting from Carl Hooper and Warne got them to 223. Allan Donald, South Africa's fastest bowler, had been rested, and Hansie Cronje took 3 for 39. South Africa's chase was no cakewalk; the hosts had Courtney Walsh as well as Warne, but after slipping to 28 for 2, the visitors made serene progress, and Jonty Rhodes's run-a-ball 111 saw them home.

The three-match Test series was a thrill, mostly for the right reasons. South Africa's emphatic opening win at Lord's was adorned by a gutsy Kepler Wessels century, and only spoiled by the strangest captaincy decision of Atherton's career: to smear the ball with a pocketful of dust (for which he gave a far-fetched explanation, that he was using the dirt to dry his hands). Hick scored a century – a rarity for him at Test level – in a draw at Leeds, before England memorably levelled the series at The Oval, where Devon Malcolm blew South Africa away with 9 for 57 in their second innings.

Further north and south

Cape Town and Chester-le-Street, 1995

The end of Apartheid meant the Queen was able to visit South Africa again. The country had been suspended from the Commonwealth in 1961, well before its exclusion from global cricket, and on its readmittance in 1994, a Royal visit was arranged. The Queen had not visited since celebrating her 21st birthday there, as HRH The Princess Elizabeth in 1947. For a week in March 1995, she was the guest of President Nelson Mandela. On the third day of her visit, she was taken to the Langa township, on the fringe of Cape Town, to watch the local children playing cricket. Black and white youngsters played scratch games on the outfield – somewhat incongruously clad in shirts bearing the name of the club's sponsor, Bakers Biscuits – while the Queen looked on.

A crowd of several hundred people, desperate to see the Queen, overwhelmed the security officials and poured onto the sports field. The Queen was whisked away quickly before anything got out of hand. "It's such a shame," a consular official told the South African press. "Hardly anyone got to see her, and she dearly would have wanted to watch the children playing."

Having visited southern Africa, later in the year – after England's series against West Indies – she made her most northerly trip. Durham had been a first-class county since 1992, but its acceptance into county cricket was conditional on the construction of a new Test-match ground. The Riverside, at Chester-le-Street, was completed in 1995 and had its grand opening on 13 October. Though it was too late in the year for any cricket, the Queen was greeted by a stand full of Durham members and officials. Having opened the ground – the only cricket ground she officially opened during her reign – she met the players and, in another first, their wives and partners.

The lucky thirteenth

London, 1997

In 1996, though India and Pakistan toured the UK, the Queen experienced her first year with no cricketing engagements since 1987, but in the New Year Honours of 1997 it was announced that Alec Bedser was to be knighted for services to cricket. He was the Queen's 13th cricketing knight. Christopher Martin-Jenkins wrote that Bedser was "the first specialist bowler" on whom she bestowed the honour, though by excluding Allen and Hadlee, Martin-Jenkins may have been stretching a point. Bedser was an England selector from 1962 to 1985, and chair of the panel from 1968 to 1981. History may not be altogether kind to his stewardship. He oversaw the controversial omission of D'Oliveira for the 1968 tour to South Africa and was later a founding member of the Freedom Association, a pressure group which advocated South Africa's return to international sport in spite of Apartheid. He was made president of Surrey in 1987, and it was for this, as much as anything else, that he received his knighthood. His investiture was at Buckingham Palace on 18 March.

The Queen had an appointment to attend every Ashes Test at Lord's since 1956, and 1997 was no exception. The plan was for her to come on the fourth day, a Sunday, but bad weather prevented her from doing so. Only 17.4 overs were possible, during which Australia added 82 for the loss of five wickets. It was the first time she had been denied any play in an Ashes game since 1972, when the match ended before she arrived at the ground. As on that occasion, she made up for it by inviting the Australians to the Palace that evening.

Cricket in the subcontinent

Pakistan v South Africa at Rawalpindi, 1997

Pakistan 456 (Azhar Mahmood 128*, Ali Naqvi 115, Mushtaq Ahmed 59) **and 182 for 6** (Inzamam-ul-Haq 56, Azhar Mahmood 50*). **South Africa 403** (G. Kirsten 98, J. H. Kallis 61, A. M. Bacher 50; Saqlain Mushtaq 5–129). **Drawn.**

In the autumn of 1997, the Queen attended a match overseas. She had knighted Sobers in Barbados in 1975, attended the Centenary Test in Australia in 1997, seen children play cricket in a South African township in 1995, and now she made a state visit to Pakistan, formerly part of the British Empire, though she had not been its monarch since 1956. She began her trip in Islamabad, where she was welcomed by President Farooq Leghari, who hosted a banquet in her honour. That evening, the Queen gave a speech noting the humanitarian work of Princess Diana, who had died a few weeks earlier. The following day, she spoke at the parliament, and met former prime minister Benazir Bhutto, before travelling to the Rawalpindi Cricket Stadium to watch the third day of the first Test between Pakistan and South Africa. It was the only time she saw a Test match not involving England.

Though it ended in a draw, it was quite a match. Pakistan won the toss and elected to bat, doing their best to see off Donald at his quickest, and the skiddy Shaun Pollock. They were 216 for 6 at the end of the first day, with no batter offering much except debutant opener Ali Naqvi, who batted nearly all day for 115. It was rare for a rookie to do so well against such a fine attack, but on the second day, lightning struck twice. Having slid to 231 for 8, Pakistan were first rescued, then rocketed into a position of dominance, by Azhar Mahmood, also playing his first Test. He added 74 with Waqar Younis for the ninth wicket and was 72 not out – with Pakistan 345 for 9 – at the end of the second day.

Third day – 8 October

No more than 700 people had come to the Rawalpindi Cricket Stadium on the first and second days, but that changed dramatically on the third, when a capacity crowd of 15,000 packed the stands in the hope of catching a glimpse of the Queen. Before she met the teams, the Pakistan fans were treated to the thrilling spectacle of Azhar Mahmood completing a century on Test debut – the second man to do so in the innings, after Ali Naqvi – during a last-wicket partnership of 151 with Mushtaq Ahmed, which equalled the world record. South Africa dropped anchor, crawling to 139 for 1 by the close. It was the last time the Queen saw South Africa play cricket.

Never before had two Test debutants scored a century in the same innings – but there were other records too. Pakistan's total more than doubled after Azhar came in at 206 for 6, and his three-hour stand of 151 with Mushtaq Ahmed – who made a career-best 59, including four sixes – equalled the Test record for the 10th wicket, set by Brian Hastings and Richard Collinge for New Zealand against Pakistan at Auckland in February 1973. Having been in the field long into the third day, the stunned South Africans were suffering from the sweltering heat and decided not to try anything risky when at last their time came to reply to Pakistan's 456. Gary Kirsten and Adam Bacher spent over three hours carefully accruing 107, then Kallis joined Kirsten to add another 114. On the fourth day, Kirsten finally fell for 98, scored over seven hours, and South Africa eked out 403 in 167.5 overs, shared between only four bowlers. The spinners, Mushtaq Ahmed and Saqlain Mushtaq, bore the brunt of the work, sharing more than 120 overs for eight wickets.

By the fifth day, it was clear the match was heading towards stalemate. The pitch had become slower by the day, and though South Africa reduced Pakistan to 80 for 5 on the final afternoon, a sprightly stand of 68 between Inzamam-ul-Haq and Azhar was sufficient to secure the draw. Torrential rain was responsible for the draw in the second Test at Sheikhupura, before a riveting decider was played out at Faisalabad, where South Africa fell to 98 for 7 before Pat Symcox hit 81 from number nine and Kirsten carried his bat for 100. Although Pakistan earned a lead, and needed just 146 to win, they were blown away for 92, Pollock taking 5 for 37.

Two more honours

Barbados, 1998

England played South Africa and Sri Lanka at home in 1998 but, as was now to be expected, the Queen did not watch either team. Stewart had taken over the captaincy from Atherton at the start of the summer, and led England to a remarkable – and somewhat unexpected – victory over South Africa. The bubble burst when Sri Lanka – now one-day world champions – pulled off a remarkable heist in a standalone Test at The Oval.

After knighthoods were bestowed upon Sobers and the three Ws, it increasingly became the habit of Caribbean countries to honour their cricketing greats. Conrad Hunte was the next to be knighted, having devoted much of his retirement to coaching in townships in South Africa, and working hard to improve race relations. He had just returned to Barbados after a period living in the USA, and was elected president of the Barbados Cricket Association on a platform of reform and reinvigoration. He was knighted by the Barbados government in 1998, but died suddenly the following year, before he could make a lasting impression on the administration of West Indian cricket. In his New Year message of 1999, Lester Bird, prime minister of Antigua, announced that his government would confer a knighthood on Viv Richards, his country's most famous son.

A carnival of cricket

London, 1999

After a wait of 16 years, the men's cricket World Cup returned to England for what was marketed as a 'carnival of cricket'. The Queen held a reception at Buckingham Palace for all the teams. For some countries, it was their final cricketing contact with her. She had seen her final India match in 1982, so this was her only chance to meet Mohammad Azharuddin, Rahul Dravid, Anil Kumble, Sourav Ganguly and Sachin Tendulkar. Her last New Zealand game was in 1986, so this reception gave the likes of Stephen Fleming and Daniel Vettori the opportunity to be introduced. And she never saw Sri Lanka or Zimbabwe play, so this was the closest she got to seeing the great Muttiah Muralitharan and Mahela Jayawardene, or Andy Flower. Roy Dias, the Sri Lanka coach, became the only cricketer from his country to meet the Queen three times (he had been in the World Cup parties of 1979 and 1983). Greenidge was the first West Indian cricketer to meet her seven times, this time in his role as coach of Bangladesh. It was the first time the Queen had met a team from Bangladesh, Kenya or Scotland.

Unlike in 1975, 1979 or 1983, the Queen attended the World Cup final in person. It had been a topsy-turvy tournament, and three of the nine Test-playing teams had been eliminated in the first group stage. West Indies, who had won the first two tournaments in the UK, were knocked out on net run-rate, and Sri Lanka could only beat Zimbabwe and Kenya and were eliminated. But the big shock was the failure of England to progress – again, it came down to run-rate. A 122-run thrashing by South Africa had been enough to sink their campaign. Australia, the dominant team of the time, came close to missing out on the semi-finals, only progressing after South Africa's Herschelle Gibbs dropped a crucial catch off Steve Waugh in their last group game. It set up a blockbuster replay between the two teams in the semi-final at Birmingham – a low-scoring thriller which went down to the last over, in which South Africa infamously choked. Australia had fought hard to reach the final, whereas Pakistan, their opponents, had romped there by topping their group and destroying New Zealand in the semis.

The showdown at Lord's was desperately one-sided. Accurate seam bowling from Glenn McGrath, Damien Fleming and Reiffel restricted the Pakistanis, while Warne tortured them with his bag of tricks. His 4 for 33 saw Pakistan bowled out for just 132, a full 11 overs short of their allocation, and made the result a formality. Despite having the great Wasim Akram and the super-fast Shoaib Akhtar in their line-up – not to mention Saqlain Mushtaq, the pioneer of the doosra – Pakistan could do nothing to hold Australia back. Mark Waugh anchored the chase, while Adam Gilchrist and Ricky Ponting went for their shots, and Australia won their second World Cup by eight wickets. It was the last time the Queen saw Pakistan play cricket. England, meanwhile, suffered a humiliating Test series defeat to New Zealand, under their new captain Nasser Hussain.

The Queen made a state visit to South Africa in late 1999, as the guest of Mbeki, who had succeeded Mandela as president. While there, on 11 November she visited the Alexandra Oval in Durban, and met Caddick and Alex Tudor, who had been left behind – deliberately – while the rest of the squad travelled to a tour match in Bloemfontein the following day.

In 2000, the exceptionally busy millennium year, Zimbabwe and West Indies toured England, but the Queen had no cricketing engagements. The year marked another change in her relationship with the sport, her attendance becoming an exception rather than the rule.

The new invincibles

England v Australia at Lord's, 2001

England 187 (G. D. McGrath 5–54) **and 227** (M. A. Butcher 83; J. N. Gillespie 5–53). **Australia 4 for 1** (M. E. Waugh 108, A. C. Gilchrist 90, D. R. Martyn 52; A. R. Caddick 5–101) **and 14 for 2. Australia won by eight wickets.**

The Queen had not seen a Test in England since 1993. In that time, she had seen an exhibition match at Highclere, a Test in Pakistan and a World Cup final at Lord's. But she had an appointment to attend every Ashes Test at Lord's since 1956, and 2001 was no exception.

Australia had by then won six series on the trot, the longest Ashes winning run since the nineteenth century. And the 2001 Australians were considered the toughest proposition yet. They certainly started the summer well, thrashing Worcestershire by 360 runs before winning a triangular one-day tournament, defeating England three times, then beating Pakistan by nine wickets at Lord's in a reprise of the 1999 World Cup final. By the time they had destroyed MCC by 280 runs, comparisons were already being drawn with Bradman's 'Invincibles' of 1948.

Australia used just 13 players in the Ashes, and only one team change was unforced. Matthew Hayden, the dominant left-hander, opened the batting with the swashbuckling Slater. Ponting, perhaps Australia's most complete batter of the decade, came in at first drop, followed by Mark Waugh, arguably their most dashing. Then came the heroic, imperturbable leader, Steve Waugh, and the elegant Damien Martyn at six. England's biggest nightmare, though, was what came next: Gilchrist, the greatest wicketkeeper-batter in the game's history, who scored runs terrifyingly quickly. The bowling attack was near-perfect. McGrath, the relentless seamer, was coupled with the express speed of Brett Lee and the pacy swing of Jason Gillespie. If you saw them off, you had to contend with Warne, the best wrist-spinner of all time.

It is a marvel that any team beat them that summer. In a one-day match, Middlesex defeated an Australia team featuring seven of the big names, and Pakistan won an ODI against a full-strength side. Midway through the Ashes, Hampshire bowled Australia out for 97 on the first day at Southampton and sneaked to victory by two wickets.

But England, after a drawn two-Test series with Pakistan, had little confidence going into the first Test at Birmingham, and delivered a patchy batting performance after Australia elected to field. After losing Marcus Trescothick for a duck, Atherton and Mark Butcher put on 104, before McGrath and Warne hit their stride, reducing the hosts to 191 for 9. But then there came another hundred partnership between Stewart and last man Caddick to take the hosts to 294. When Australia were 134 for 3, England's looked a respectable total. Reality soon dawned, though. Steve Waugh and Martyn each scored 105, and when the fifth wicket fell at 336, it only brought in Gilchrist, who walloped 152 off 143. Facing a deficit of 282, England reached 99 for 1 before being swept away for 164. To make things worse they lost their captain, Nasser Hussain, to a broken finger. Atherton, who had stepped down as England captain in 1998, took the reins for the next two Tests.

First day – 19 July

To no one's surprise, it rained when the Queen visited Lord's on the opening day. Put in to bat, England struggled against Jason Gillespie and Glenn McGrath, and were 121 for 4 when play ended early.

The Queen visited the first day of the Lord's Test. The start was delayed by rain for an hour and a half, whereupon England were asked to bat. Trescothick was caught behind off Gillespie, then McGrath removed Butcher, Thorpe and Atherton, before the day's play ended early at 121 for 4. They made it to 187 on the second day, with McGrath taking 5 for 54, and Australia had already taken the lead by the close. Mark Waugh's century put them 214 ahead, and Gillespie's 5 for 53 ensured the visitors chased only a very small target.

In the third Test, England were dismantled again, despite keeping Australia to a first-innings lead of just five. McGrath in the first innings (5 for 49) and Warne in the second (6 for 33) made sure the Ashes would stay Down Under. Hussain returned to lead England at Leeds, where Australia handed a debut to Simon Katich while Steve Waugh rested a strained leg muscle. Gilchrist captained in his stead and, after Ponting's 144, Martyn's 118 and McGrath's 7 for 76 had helped give Australia a lead of 138, he could not resist setting England a tempting target of 314 from 110 overs, so keen was he to win the series 5–0. It looked like business as usual when England slipped to 33 for 2, but Butcher batted like a man possessed, striking 173 off 227 to bring the hosts home by six wickets. Normal service was resumed at The Oval, however, when Steve Waugh – still struggling with a leg injury – returned to score a heroic unbeaten 157 in Australia's mammoth 641 for 4. Despite Mark Ramprakash's 133, England fell 10 runs short of avoiding the follow on. McGrath then took 5 for 43, and Warne 4 for 64, as England's collective willpower was exhausted, and they slumped to an innings defeat.

At the Academy

Loughborough, 2003

The Queen didn't attend any cricket in 2002, when Sri Lanka and India toured England, and though she watched no matches the following year either (when Zimbabwe and South Africa came), she did have an engagement with the England and Wales Cricket Board. On 14 November 2003, along with the Duke of Edinburgh, she opened the National Cricket Academy at Loughborough University. She was accompanied by various dignitaries from the county of Leicestershire, as well as from the university, and was presented with flowers by Bethan and Emily, the daughters of Hugh Morris, performance director at the ECB.

On her tour of the facility, she was shown the Hawk-Eye ball-tracking system, the super slow-motion camera, and the state-of-the-art strength and conditioning room. Finally, she was brought to the main hall to meet Boycott (for the 12th time, which remained the record for an England cricketer), and to watch net practice, with commentary from Jonathan Agnew, the BBC's cricket correspondent.

The magnificent seven

England v West Indies at Lord's, 2004

England 568 (R. W. T. Key 221, A. J. Strauss 137, M. P. Vaughan 103; P. T. Collins 4–113) **and 325 for 5 declared** (M. P. Vaughan 101*, A. Flintoff 58). **West Indies 416** (S. Chanderpaul 128*, C. H. Gayle 66; A. F. Giles 4–129) **and 267** (S. Chanderpaul 97*, C. H. Gayle 81; A. F. Giles 5–81). **England won by 210 runs.**

England's golden summer started at Lord's in the first Test against New Zealand. The Kiwis, on the back of 93 and 101 from Mark Richardson, set England 282 to win and, as they marched to their target, Andrew Strauss looked like reaching twin hundreds on debut. But Hussain ran him out for 83, before making amends with a century of his own, and then retired from international cricket after the match. In the second Test at Headingley, Trescothick and Geraint Jones scored hundreds as England took a lead of 117, and their developing pace attack of Steve Harmison, Matthew Hoggard and Andrew Flintoff then bowled New Zealand out for 161 to ensure an easy chase. The visitors, powered by 117 from Fleming and 108 from Scott Styris, managed to get a lead in the third Test at Trent Bridge and set England 284 to win, only for Thorpe to see the hosts home with an unbeaten 104. England had three Test wins under their belt by the middle of June.

Next came the turn of West Indies, and the omens were not good for them. They lost to Ireland at Stormont, and though they beat England twice in the triangular one-day series, they could not get the better of New Zealand, in the group or in the final. But as the Test series approached, they turned the corner with the bat: Devon Smith and Brian Lara, the captain, scored hundreds against MCC, and Sylvester Joseph, Dwayne Bravo, Ridley Jacobs and Shivnarine Chanderpaul did likewise against Sri Lanka A. The worry was their bowling – they had exhausted their conveyor belt of top-class fast bowlers following the retirements of Curtly Ambrose and Courtney Walsh.

First day – 22 July

The Queen saw England capitalise on a batting paradise against a weak West Indian attack. Andrew Strauss and Rob Key hit centuries in a stand worth 291, and England made 391 for 2 in less than 85 overs.

No one was surprised when England put West Indies to the sword at Lord's. They plundered runs on the first day, reaching 391 for 2 inside 85 overs, with Strauss making 137 and Rob Key reaching the close on 167, which he turned into 221 next day. Michael Vaughan, now England's captain, carried on where Strauss had left off, stroking a sublime 103, and England's fourth wicket did not fall until 527. Somewhat miraculously, West Indies' pop-gun attack, which had gone for more than four an over, took the last six for 41.

Having conceded 568, the visitors were reassured that at least they had batting quality. Chris Gayle raced to 66 off 82, and though Lara was caught behind off Ashley Giles for 11, Chanderpaul got his side to 208 for 4 at stumps on the third day, eventually finishing unbeaten on 128, made in six and a half hours. England were 152 ahead on first innings, and went hell for leather in the second, again scoring at more than four an over. Flintoff blasted a half-century, and Vaughan declared when he reached his second hundred of the match. The second West Indian innings went a similar way to the first. Gayle smashed 81 out of the first 102, Giles got Lara (for 44 this time), and Chanderpaul dropped anchor. Victory was never on the cards, but Chanderpaul did his best to salvage a draw, only to run out of partners. When Flintoff took the final wicket, he was left not out again, this time for 97. He had batted over 10 hours in the match for 225 runs, without being dismissed.

A pattern was set for the series: West Indies just did not have the bowling. In the second Test at Birmingham, England racked up 566 for 9 declared. Trescothick's 105 was aggressive, but Flintoff's 167 off 191 balls – with seven sixes – was another matter entirely. Ramnaresh Sarwan's 139, and Lara's beautifully fluent 95, took West Indies to 336, and England chose not to enforce the follow-on. Trescothick emulated Vaughan's feat at Lord's by adding a second hundred, and West Indies resorted to the part-time off-breaks of Chris Gayle. They worked, too: he took 5 for 34, before setting off like a rocket in pursuit of an unlikely 479. He appeared on course to take five wickets and score a century on the same day until he was undone by Giles for 82. There was little fight thereafter as Giles took 5 for 57, putting England 2–0 up.

By now, Vaughan's side were irresistible. A second-day washout in the third Test at Manchester persuaded West Indies to declare at 395 for 9 in hope of forcing a victory, and by the fourth day they had gained a lead of 65, despite Thorpe's 114. The hero was Dwayne Bravo, whose 6 for 55 remained his best Test figures. At 88 for 1, West Indies were in a promising position, 153 ahead. But nine wickets fell for 77 as Giles again worked effectively in tandem with England's seamers. The hosts needed 231 to win, and Key's unbeaten 93 got them home. In the final Test at The Oval, every England batter made double figures, and Harmison skittled West Indies with 6 for 46. The tourists followed on, and though Gayle finally made the century he'd deserved all series, England won by 10 wickets on the third day, clinching their seventh victory in seven Tests. Having won at The Oval in 2003, they made it 10 home wins in a row by beating Pakistan in the first two Tests of 2005.

Men and women honoured

London, 2005

Though the women's teams did not officially play for the Ashes until 1998, England and Australia had faced each other in Tests since 1934. Since the summer of 1989, Australia had a firm grasp on both the men's and women's trophies. The sense of achievement when England won both Ashes series in the summer of 2005 cannot be exaggerated. The women won 1–0, and the men won 3–1; the dual success was confirmed at The Oval on 12 September, when Kevin Pietersen's outrageous 158 sealed the series.

The Queen had not visited Lord's for the Ashes Test of 2005 but, like millions of people around the country, she watched the men's Ashes avidly on television, and joined in the celebrations when England triumphed. She sent a message to Vaughan: "Warmest congratulations to you, the England team and all in the squad for the magnificent achievement of regaining the Ashes. This has been a truly memorable series and both sides can take credit for giving us all such a wonderfully exciting and entertaining summer of cricket at its best."

To the Palace victorious

London, 2006

Buckingham Palace announced that the England men's team would receive New Year Honours. There were OBEs for Vaughan, the captain, and Duncan Fletcher, the coach, and MBEs for everyone else who played in the Tests – including Paul Collingwood, who only featured at The Oval, scoring 7 and 10. The chairman of selectors, David Graveney, and the team's operations managers, Phil Neale and Medha Laud, also received honours. Given the mood of generosity, it was unfortunate that, of England's women, only Clare Connor, the captain, was recognised. She received an OBE, but none of her 12 teammates were honoured. Charlotte Edwards was made an MBE in 2009, Claire Taylor in 2010 and Jenny Gunn in 2014, but the likes of Katherine Brunt – who also helped England win the World Cup in 2017 – were not honoured during the Queen's reign.

All the England players – men and women – were invited to the Picture Gallery at Buckingham Palace for a special reception on 9 February 2006. She told Vaughan that she had watched as much of the series as she could, "but not all the time, because it all became too tense". Strauss seemed more anxious about the visit to the Palace than the Ashes itself. "It was nerve-wracking going in there," he said. "Worse than going out to bat. You are half expecting someone to do something wrong, and trying to make sure it isn't you." He may have been recalling the infamous visit to 10 Downing Street in 2005, when Flintoff was so drunk he reportedly urinated in the back garden. "We're sober this time," Hoggard reassured the press. The Queen made a special effort to speak with Collingwood. "She knew I was called in for the last match and ended up in the thick of it," he said. "I was surprised how much she knew about it all."

A first look at Cook

England v West Indies at Lord's, 2007

England 553 for 5 declared (M. J. Prior 126*, P. D. Collingwood 111, I. R. Bell 109*, A. N. Cook 105) **and 284 for 8 declared** (K. P. Pietersen 109, A. N. Cook 65). **West Indies 437** (S. Chanderpaul 74, D. Ramdin 60, D. J. Bravo 56; M. S. Panesar 6–129) **and 89 for 0. Match drawn.**

The comedown from England's Ashes party was brutal. Vaughan was injured, so Flintoff stood in as captain. In 2005/06, they lost a Test series in Pakistan, but rallied to draw in India. Back home, they drew with a Muralitharan-inspired Sri Lanka, then beat Pakistan on the back of a controversial forfeit by the visitors at The Oval. Penalised for ball-tampering, Inzamam's team refused to take the field, and the umpires awarded the match – and thus the series – to England. They were then whitewashed in the 2006/07 Ashes by a rampant Australia, still powered by their awesome core: Hayden, Langer, Ponting, Gilchrist, Warne, Lee and McGrath.

Vaughan was fit again for the visits of West Indies and India in the summer of 2007. Tests against West Indies were a soft start by then: Lara had retired, leaving Chanderpaul and Gayle to carry a team of greenhorns. Few gave the visitors, captained by Sarwan, much of a chance.

First day – 17 May

On a cloudy, rainy day at Lord's, England were invited to bat, and filled their boots. Andrew Strauss and Kevin Pietersen offered support to the headline act, Alastair Cook, who made his fifth Test hundred at the age of 22. Interruptions for bad light hampered the afternoon's play, and England reached 200 for 3 by the close.

It was a good toss to lose. Overhead conditions tempted Sarwan to put England in, but the Lord's pitch was true, and only Owais Shah failed. Strauss and Cook began with 88, and though Daren Powell removed Strauss and Shah in quick succession, England gathered runs with few alarms. Pietersen's jaunty 26 was ended by Corey Collymore, which made it 162 for 3, but he was the last home batter not to reach three figures in the innings. Cook made it to his century by stumps, and on the second day his feat was equalled by Paul Collingwood, Ian Bell and Matt Prior, who became the first England wicketkeeper to score a century on debut. The speed of his scoring – his unbeaten 126 came at nearly a run a ball – enabled Strauss to declare overnight, but West Indies batted fearlessly on the third and fourth days, reaching 437. Though no batter scored a hundred, every player bar last man Collymore reached double figures. Gayle got things going with a rapid 30, and Dinesh Ramdin took his team past the follow-on mark with an assertive 60. Chanderpaul was, as so often, the linchpin, accumulating 74 in four and a half hours. England needed to score quickly to build on their lead of 116, and had just the man for the job. Pietersen's 109 made him England's fifth centurion of the match, a feat only achieved twice before in Tests, by Australia at Kingston in 1954/55 and by Pakistan at Multan in 2001/02. A second declaration set West Indies 401 on the final day, but more bad weather restricted play to 22 overs, in which England failed to take a wicket.

It rained again at Leeds, but England needed only three days of play to cast West Indies aside. They piled on the runs, with Vaughan's 103 and Pietersen's 226 driving them to 570 for 7 declared inside two days. Ryan Sidebottom took four wickets in each innings as the visitors were dismissed for 146 and 141. To make matters worse, they lost Sarwan to a shoulder injury. Daren Ganga captained at Manchester, where England won again, but there was more fight from the visitors this time. Bell's 97 got the hosts up to 370, and they took a healthy lead of 141 after Monty Panesar's 4 for 40. When England were 221 for 2 in their second innings, with Cook on the way to another century, West Indies looked utterly lost, but debutant Daren Sammy, the first St Lucian to play Test cricket, lifted spirits with 7 for 66. West Indies needed 455, and seemed destined to lose at 88 for 3, only for Chanderpaul – who had scored 50 in the first innings – to play another of his remarkable rearguards. Over seven hours, he painstakingly made an unbeaten 116, and for a time on the last morning it looked like he might engineer a win. But Panesar swept through the lower order, his 6 for 137 completing a 10-wicket match haul.

By the time they got to The Oval, West Indies seemed to have lost their spirit. England put them in, and Sidebottom took 5 for 88; only Chanderpaul, with 136 not out, had an appetite for the battle. England took a lead of 113 through Collingwood's 128, though Fidel Edwards claimed a fast and furious 5 for 112. Chanderpaul's 70 held England up again but another haul from Panesar (5 for 46) set up a seven-wicket win for the hosts. The season didn't go all their way, though: India won the late-summer series 1–0.

England's quartet calls the tune

England v Australia at Lord's, 2009

England 425 (A. J. Strauss 161, A. N. Cook 95; B. W. Hilfenhaus 4–103) **and 311 for 6 declared** (M. J. Prior 61, P. D. Collingwood 54). **Australia 215** (M. E. K. Hussey 51; J. M. Anderson 4–55) **and 406** (M. J. Clarke 136, B. J. Haddin 80, M. G. Johnson 63; A. Flintoff 5–92, G. P. Swann 4–87). **England won by 115 runs.**

England continued to take one step forward, and one step back. New Zealand came to England in 2008, and were bested by Sidebottom and Pietersen. Panesar, too, continued to pose problems, and James Anderson took 7 for 43 at Nottingham. But then came the visit of South Africa, and England were on the back foot again. The visitors scored heavily, and England came unstuck against the pacy swing of Dale Steyn and the steepling bounce of Morne Morkel. Vaughan gave up the captaincy, and Pietersen was appointed to the role for the final Test at The Oval, inspiring England to a consolation victory. He didn't last long in the job: that winter, a rift developed between Pietersen and the coach, Peter Moores, and both were sacked. England installed a new regime: Strauss as captain, and Andy Flower as coach. They didn't get off to a good start. England were bowled out for 51 in Jamaica, and though they gave a better account of themselves in later games – and discovered a fine off-spinner in Graeme Swann – a succession of draws handed West Indies a shock series win.

A couple of comfortable home victories against the same opposition in May 2009 put England in a better mood ahead of the Ashes, and a close contest was anticipated. In the first Test in Cardiff, England posted 435 and saw little to unsettle them from Mitchell Johnson, Ben Hilfenhaus or Peter Siddle. And – heaven be praised – Warne was gone, succeeded by the near-anonymous Nathan Hauritz. But England's attack proved even more toothless. Anderson, Stuart

Broad, Flintoff, Panesar and Swann were a wonderful quintet on paper, but Australia panned them for 674. Four batters – Katich, Ponting, Marcus North and Brad Haddin – made centuries, and England were confronted with the real possibility of an innings defeat after they slumped to 70 for 5 on the last morning. But Collingwood resisted for nearly six hours, before Anderson and Panesar held out for 69 balls.

Despite his heroics, Panesar was dropped for the second Test, with Graham Onions taking his place. England had another good first day, Strauss batting throughout for 161. The hosts were 364 for 6 at the close.

Second day – 17 July

After a sprightly last-wicket stand of 45 between James Anderson and Graham Onions, England's bowlers laboured against Simon Katich and Mike Hussey, who took Australia to 103 for 2 in response to the hosts' 425. But the pace quartet – James Anderson, Andrew Flintoff, Stuart Broad and Graham Onions – had a joyous afternoon, taking 6 for 49 between them, and Australia were perilously placed on 156 for 8 at stumps.

Strauss was bowled second ball next morning; Broad and Swann soon followed. Though Anderson and Onions added 45 for the last wicket, England's 425 felt like a missed opportunity. Anderson quickly removed Phil Hughes and Ponting, but Katich and Mike Hussey took the score to 103 for 2, and England looked jittery. Everything changed when Katich was brilliantly caught on the hook by Broad at long leg, starting a match-defining collapse. Hussey was bowled by Flintoff, and Anderson dismissed Michael Clarke next over. North was Anderson's fourth victim, then Broad got rid of Johnson and Haddin. Australia were 156 for 8 at the end of the day, and the game already felt like England's.

Hauritz and Siddle got Australia up to 215, and England batted again, 210 ahead. Half-centuries from Collingwood and Prior set Australia 521 in two days, and after they had slid to 128 for 5, Clarke and Haddin recovered the situation so well that there was a feeling they might conjure a victory on the final day. They needed 208, with five wickets in hand, and HRH Princess Anne was there to see if they could do it. But Swann produced a beauty which broke back through Clarke's gate, and Flintoff bowled himself into the ground at the other end, to make sure Australia never got close. Rain at Birmingham saw the third Test end in a draw, and Australia levelled the series with a potent seam-bowling performance in the fourth Test at Leeds. The teams were therefore all square going to The Oval, and the Ashes had a bona fide decider for the first time since Melbourne in 1966. Broad's magic second-day spell, and Jonathan Trott's debut hundred, brought the urn back to England.

From Lord's to the Lords

London, 2011

By 2010, the Queen and her Commonwealth had appointed 16 cricketing knights – the most recent being Ian Botham in 2007 – and three lords. The first, Learie Constantine, was a true polymath. Born in Trinidad, he played regularly for West Indies in the twenties and thirties, and for Nelson in the Lancashire League. During the War, he helped organise West Indian workers in British factories, and played an important role in improving race relations, latterly as a barrister, then as Trinidad and Tobago's High Commissioner in London. He was knighted in 1962, and became Baron Constantine of Nelson in 1969. Cowdrey was elevated to the peerage in 1997, becoming Baron Cowdrey of Tonbridge, and David Sheppard became Baron Sheppard of Liverpool – having been appointed Bishop of Liverpool in 1975 – shortly after his retirement, in 1998.

A total of 17, then, and nary a woman among them. That lop-sided distribution took a small step towards being rectified on 19 November 2010, when Downing Street announced that the Queen would confer the first peerage on a female cricketer. Rachael Heyhoe Flint had played 22 Tests and 23 one-day internationals for England between 1960 and 1982, captaining the team for 12 of those years. She hit the first six in a women's Test, at The Oval against Australia in 1963, and was the driving force behind the creation of the cricket World Cup, which began in 1973 with a women's tournament in England. Though she had argued strongly in favour of the South African tour of 1970 during Apartheid, writing in her autobiography that it was "hardly the place of any English people to criticise", she was undeniably a force for good in cricket, and the women's game in particular. In 1999, she became one of the first 10 women admitted to MCC, and in 2010 she was the first woman to be inducted into the ICC's Cricket Hall of Fame.

Prime minister David Cameron telephoned her with the news that the Queen would be appointing her a life peer, as Baroness Heyhoe Flint of Wolverhampton. "I was completely surprised," she said.

150

"Obviously I am really thrilled, but still very humbled at the thought of joining such an historic institution." Elevated as a Conservative peer at the beginning of 2011, she made 34 speeches in the House of Lords, over five years from 2011 to 2016, on subjects such as children's participation in sport, ticket touting, disabled spectators and the Olympic games. Her last speech, about corruption and cheating, was on 3 May 2016; she died eight months later.

A pillar of the Caribbean
Barbados, 2012

Barbados loves cricketing knighthoods. After the Queen had knighted Frank Worrell in the 1964 New Year Honours, and Garry Sobers at the Garrison Savannah in 1975, the government of Barbados had bestowed its own knighthoods on Clyde Walcott in 1993, Everton Weekes in 1995 and Conrad Hunte in 1998. The sixth son of the island to be dubbed was Wes Hall, the man who took West Indies' first hat-trick, who bowled the final over of the first tied Test, and who broke Cowdrey's arm at Lord's. After his retirement, Hall was a West Indies team manager, chair of selectors and president of the board. It was on account of Hall that the World Cup came to the Caribbean in 2007. The great cricket writer C. L. R. James once said: "Hall simply exudes good nature at every pore." He was part of the first great West Indian fast bowling combination, with fellow Barbadian Charlie Griffith, and though his knighthood was widely welcomed on the island, many regarded the job as only half done.

The final Test

England v Australia at Lord's, 2013

England 361 (I. R. Bell 109, J. M. Bairstow 67, I. J. L. Trott 58; R. J. Harris 5–72) **and 349 for 7 declared** (J. E. Root 180, I. R. Bell 75). **Australia 128** (G. P. Swann 5–44) **and 235** (U. T. Khawaja 54, M. J. Clarke 51; G. P. Swann 4–78). **England won by 347 runs.**

England's four years from 2010 to 2013 were among the best the Test team had ever known. After the 2009 Ashes, they drew a series in South Africa, then trounced Bangladesh away and at home. In the second half of the summer of 2010, they defeated Pakistan, before embarking on a successful tour of Australia, winning the Ashes abroad for the first time in more than a quarter of a century. In 2011, their defeats of Sri Lanka and India took them to the top of the Test tree, and though they were whitewashed by Pakistan in the United Arab Emirates the following winter, they triumphed in Sri Lanka. West Indies were beaten in the summer of 2012, but South Africa again proved impossible to crack. Strauss announced his retirement, but under Alastair Cook, England emerged triumphant from the hardest assignment of all, a Test tour of India, in 2012/13. After two series against New Zealand – drawing away, victorious at home – it was time for another Ashes battle.

The first Test at Nottingham was a classic, twisting and turning unpredictably. England chose to bat and were bowled out for 215 on the first day, with Siddle claiming 5 for 50. Anderson reduced Australia to 117 for 9 in reply, despite a half-century from Steve Smith, bringing debutant number eleven Ashton Agar to the middle. Astonishingly, he not only stuck around, but started smashing the ball around the ground, putting on a scarcely believable 163 for the last wicket with Phil Hughes. He was caught in the deep going for his century; 98 was the highest score ever made by a No. 11 in a Test, and it gave Australia a lead of 65. England were on a slippery slope at 174 for 5, but Bell saved them with an elegant 109, setting Australia 311. Though they reached 111 for 1, another collapse left them on the brink at 231 for 9. Agar, promoted to number eight, made 14, and the new man at No. 11, James Pattinson, helped Haddin nudge Australia closer to victory. But finally, with just 15 needed, Haddin nicked Anderson behind, giving him his 10th wicket of the match – and England a lead in the series.

First day – 18 July

The Queen's final day at the cricket was a close, keenly-fought affair. Ryan Harris bowled manfully, and England were 28 for 3 before Ian Bell's glorious 109 took them into the ascendancy. Jonathan Trott made 58 and Jonny Bairstow struck 67 before Steve Smith's occasional leg-spin claimed 3 for 18, balancing the day's play, with England 289 for 7.

Batting first at Lord's, England quickly lost Cook, Joe Root and Pietersen, as Ryan Harris, the Australian fast bowler, hit his straps. But Trott and Jonny Bairstow scored half-centuries while Bell gathered runs attractively. He saved England with his second 109 in succession, putting on 99 with Trott and 144 with Bairstow. Though all three, and Prior, were gone by the close – Smith's leg-breaks were unexpectedly pressed into action and brought him 3 for 18, the best figures of his Test career – England had recovered to 289 for 7 at stumps.

Beefy hitting from Broad and Swann upped the total to 361 on the second morning, before Australia capitulated in the face of masterful off-spin from Swann. Varying his flight intelligently, he claimed 5 for 44 and bowled Australia out for 128. England had a lead of 233 but decided to bat again so that Swann could bowl in the final innings. Rather carelessly, they were 31 for 3 at the close. Bell hit a classy 74 next day, but Root stole the show. Watchful at first, he put together a smart century, before hitting out with merry abandon as the lead swelled. Cook finally declared at 347, setting Australia 582 in nearly three days. It was only a matter of time for England, and they did it in a day. Australia were woeful against spin again, Swann talking 4 for 78 and Root's part-time off-breaks claiming 2 for 9. England went 2–0 up in the blink of an eye.

Australia were denied by the Manchester rain in the third Test. Clarke's 187 had helped them reach 527, and England were soon chasing the game. Despite Pietersen's 113, they conceded a lead of 159, and Australia went hell for leather to set up a declaration. England needed 332 from 98 overs on the final day, and crawled to 37 for 3 when the rain curtailed the contest. Had the weather not intervened, Australia would surely have levelled the series. They were ahead on first innings in the fourth Test, too, with Chris Rogers's 110 helping them to 270 in reply to England's 238. But Bell was England's hero once again. While Harris charged in, claiming 7 for 117, Bell stroked a crucial 113 to set Australia 299. With David Warner on the offensive, the visitors reached 168 for 2, but his dismissal sparked a procession, with Broad putting in one of his famous spells. He finished with 6 for 50 as England retained the Ashes with a game to spare. They nearly won the fifth Test at The Oval too, after Clarke's sporting declaration set them 227 in 44 overs. They had reduced the equation to 21 from four overs when the umpires decided the light was too bad to continue. Cook became the third England captain to lift the Ashes at home since the turn of the century.

Three knights in one day

Antigua, 2014

Having knighted Viv Richards just before turn of the century, the Antiguan government similarly honoured three more of its finest players in 2014, bringing the number of West Indian cricketing knights to 11. The investiture, by Governor General Louise Lake-Tack, was held during the lunch interval of a one-day international between West Indies and England at St John's on 28 February.

Andy Roberts played 103 times for West Indies, including 47 Tests. He was perhaps the most brutal of the famous pace quartet of the late seventies, with his ingenious and unsettling ploy of bowling two bouncers in succession, the second much faster than the first. After his retirement, he became a key figure in improving Caribbean pitches, and coached pace bowlers around the world.

Richie Richardson took on the West Indies captaincy after the retirement of Viv Richards. It was an unenviable task, as his tenure coincided with the irresistible rise of Australia. A flamboyant and indomitable batter, he retired within a year of the watershed defeat to the Australians in 1994/95, with over 10,000 international runs to his name. The most potent weapon in his team – and his band-mate in Big Bad Dread and the Baldhead, the Antiguan reggae group – was the fast bowler Curtly Ambrose, who was knighted alongside him. Ambrose, in tandem with his new-ball partner Courtney Walsh, was perhaps the leading fast bowler of the nineties; many say he was the last truly great West Indian fast bowler, though that may be a little harsh on Kemar Roach. Ambrose put genuine terror into the hearts of opposing batters, not least at Trinidad in 1993/94, when he bowled England out for 46.

Two greats united

Barbados, 2017

If Ambrose and Walsh were the last great West Indian new-ball pair, Hall and Griffith were the first. Five years after Hall was knighted, the business many Barbadians had considered unfinished was completed by the investiture of his new-ball partner, Charlie Griffith. He took 94 Test wickets, compared with Hall's 192, and had been the subject of some controversy during his playing days. In 1962, he fractured the skull of India captain Nari Contractor with a bouncer, ending his playing career; he was no-balled for throwing in the same Test, as he was in England four years later. But in Barbados he was both a big name and a loyal servant. In 1988, the Kensington Oval opened the Hall and Griffith Stand.

A toast to Cook

London, 2019

The first cricketer to continue playing professional, competitive cricket after receiving his knighthood was the 22nd to be so honoured by the Queen: Alastair Cook, the first since Botham to be personally dubbed by the monarch. By any measure he was a great of the English game, having broken several national Test records, including most appearances, most runs and most matches as captain. He achieved a world record too, playing 159 consecutive Tests. Cook announced his retirement ahead of the final Test of the 2018 summer, against India at The Oval. He made 71 and 147, as England won the match and the series. On 28 December, he was listed for a knighthood in the New Year Honours, and the investiture took place at the Palace on 26 February 2019. Cook was still playing for Essex three years later.

The Queen's last reception

London, 2019

England held its fifth men's World Cup in 2019 and, on the eve of the tournament, the Queen hosted her traditional reception. On this occasion, the invitation was extended to captains only, presumably because circulating between 150 players, all eager to meet her, was considered rather too much for a 93-year-old monarch. It was an intimate affair, as the Queen shook hands with the 10 captains, most of whom looked more like bashful schoolboys than international athletes. None more so than Gulbadin Naib, who could not stop grinning with the thrill of it all. Jason Holder, all six feet seven of him, bowed his head so low he looked like he might rick his neck.

In days gone by, the Palace issued advice on how to dress for an audience with the Queen. This had become a little less prescriptive with time. Faf du Plessis, though indoors, wore a scarf in South African colours. Virat Kohli committed an even greater *faux pas*, wearing a dark navy suit, at least a size too small, with light brown shoes.

There are those, not least among anti-monarchists, who suggest that the Queen's life was one of idle pleasure at the expense of her subjects. Her diary for 29 May 2019 would be a revelation to them. Before the reception with the World Cup captains, she had already had three meetings. The first was with Carol Ann Duffy, to accept her relinquishment of the post of Poet Laureate. The next was with Simon Armitage, to confer the post on him, and to present him with the Queen's Gold Medal for Poetry. Then she met Lieutenant General Rick Evraire of the Canadian armed forces. After the World Cup reception, she hosted a garden party; these huge events, for members of the public who had performed some notable deed in their community, usually had about 8,000 guests. When the party was concluded, she had her weekly audience with the prime minster, Theresa May. This was a typical day for a woman in her 94th year.

Three final appointments

London, 2020

The Queen's last three cricketing appointments were not in person. The first was on St Valentine's Day in 2020 when she conferred the knighthood bestowed, in prime minister Theresa May's Resignation Honours, on Geoffrey Boycott. He was the 23rd cricketer to be knighted during her reign, and was dubbed at the Palace by HRH Prince Charles.

Botham was elevated to the peerage the same summer, becoming Baron Botham of Ravensworth, the Queen's fifth cricketing peer. There had only been four before her reign, and all had inherited their titles: George, Lord Harris; Martin, Lord Hawke; Lionel, Lord Tennyson; and Ivo Bligh, the Earl of Darnley. That made Learie Constantine's life peerage in 1969 particularly special: the first cricketer to be ennobled by the Queen was black. So too was the last cricketer on whom she conferred a knighthood: Clive Lloyd, who was named in the 2020 New Year Honours, and dubbed by HRH Prince William in January 2022.

Her Majesty Queen Elizabeth II died of old age at 3.10pm on Thursday 8 September 2022 at Balmoral Castle, with HRH Prince Charles and HRH Princess Anne by her side. During the period of national mourning that followed, her coffin lay in state at Westminster Hall. More than 250,000 people queued for up to 10 miles and 24 hours to pay their respects. The funeral was attended by 73 foreign heads of state, and a million people lined the streets of London for the procession. Queen Elizabeth reigned for 70 years and 214 days, during which 10,973 official international cricket matches took place – 94.3 per cent of the total ever played.